MOTIVATION MATTERS

REVOLUTIONISE YOUR WRITING ONE
CREATIVE STEP AT A TIME

WENDY H. JONES

*All the very best with
your own writing
Wendy H. Jones*

SCOTT AND LAWSON

www.wendyhjones.com

Cover design by Cathy Helms of Avalon Graphics LLC

ISBN: 978-0-9956457-6-9

To each and every author who is reading this book, for working tire-lessly to bring your books to fruition. You are all heroes.

ACKNOWLEDGMENTS

All the members of City Writers, Dundee, for your untiring advice, patience and support whilst I wrote this book.

Thank you to Sheena McLeod and Chris Longmuir, for all their support with proofing and editing.

CONTENTS

INTRODUCTION

A s a writer myself, I know how important motivation is to the writing process. Yet, recently I have heard many writers, of all stages of the journey, say they just can't get motivated to write. Their get up and go seems to have not only got up and gone but emigrated. I can understand this. Life in modern times seems to be crazy busy and often-times writing can seem like an uphill battle.

PEOPLE OFTEN ASK ME, "How do you get so much done? How do you stay motivated?"

These are both good questions and I intend to answer them. Firstly, I should explain, I am writing this introduction on the Island of St Kitts in the Caribbean. Currently on a cruise, I have stopped for lunch ashore. Now at the coffee stage, I am choosing to spend my time writing for fifteen minutes, bathed in glorious sunshine. This is not a bid to make you jealous but to explain what motivates me to spend time writing rather than soaking up the view. I should point out, before you accuse me of wasting an extremely nice holiday, I did watch the world go by whilst I actually ate my lunch. My motivation is knowing this book is needed. That it will help you, the writer.

AND HELP YOU IT WILL. The tried and tested strategies in this book will motivate and inspire you to pick up a pen, or crack open your laptop, and write. It will allow you to think differently and give your writing a much-needed kickstart. Think of it as your very own motivational bomb. The friendliest, and most helpful, bomb you will ever meet, so get ready to detonate an explosion in your brain.

~

How to Use this Book

WITHIN ITS PAGES lie 366 glorious invitations to change the way you think and feel about your writing. One for every day of the year, including a spare one for a leap year. However, there is no need to wait until January to start this new journey. It is designed to use now. Yes, that's right – now. This is the perfect time to explore its pages and revolutionise your writing journey. Exciting times lie ahead, both within the book and for you as a writer. Ready, steady, start now.

HOW YOU APPROACH this is entirely up to you. You can, of course, start at number 1 and work your way through the book until you reach 366. Some days you might find that particular motivational activity isn't quite right for you. Feel free to move on and return at a later date. Or you can use it as a lucky dip and drop in and out of the days. Whatever works for you. Each chapter contains one week of exercises grouped together to make it easier for you to keep track.

Whichever way you approach it, the important thing is to engage in the motivational activities, if you want to get the most from the book. Some may take you out of your comfort zone; as they do me. This is a good thing. These stretch you and allow your brain to think differently, to take you in new, exciting directions. Think of the endless possibilities awaiting you on this journey.

Before you start, buy a nice notebook. Use it to jot down notes and ideas as they come to you during the exercises. You can use these to motivate you if you feel things are slipping. You can also use them in your WIP. Two for the price of one. Bonus.

2

What Motivates Us?

I t is generally agreed motivation can be intrinsic (driven by ourselves because we find it gratifying) or extrinsic (driven by external factors such as reward). In the long term, intrinsic motivation works better. This is what allows you to keep going, even if book sales, and thus your income, fluctuate. It is what allows you to keep going when you feel like you are wading through treacle as you write.

OF COURSE, external motivation is important. Getting a nice review on your latest blockbuster, pocketing a nice fat cheque, and a queue of people at your book signing is definitely enough to motivate you. However, these can also have the opposite effect. A lukewarm review, a lacklustre royalty cheque, or few people at a signing can be demotivating.

THEREFORE, intrinsic motivation is crucial for long-term success as an author, or indeed any other career. So why is your brain sabotaging a daily writing habit? Why is it coming up with a myriad different excuses and finding other, more engrossing, things for you to do? This is the time when your house is spotless, everything is in its place and you've taken to playing online games rather than sitting down at the keyboard, or with a pencil in hand, writing?

HAVE YOU HEARD THE SAYING, "If you always do what you've always done, you'll always get what you've always got?"

USUALLY, we are demotivated because our brain is saying, it's time for a change. Let's shake it up a little and get this party jumping. This means you need to develop motivational techniques which will get your manuscript, or project, moving.

LUCKILY, you've bought this book and taken the first step. Now, follow me and let me lead you on a journey which will change how you think and drag your writing mojo back to the party, whooping and a hollering and raring to go. It's time to fill your brain to overflowing from the creative river, starting today.

∾

Rest and Relaxation

ONE OF THE main reasons why we feel demotivated is because our creative reservoir has completely dried up. Like a real reservoir, the creative version requires creative rain to fill it, keep it full and ready to perform. Yet, we writers mostly plough on, day after day, week after week, without taking time to rest, relax and refill.

TODAY, challenge yourself to step away from the keyboard, or pen and paper. Forget about writing for the day. I'm sure you are wondering what on earth I'm saying. Tell you to stop writing in order to motivate you. Yes, that's exactly what I'm saying. Take a day off. Do something you enjoy. Do something that makes you feel good. Read a book, spend time with friends, go out for lunch, pamper yourself with a massage. Whatever it is, take time to enjoy the day.

BUT, I hear you say, I've a deadline approaching. I need to get my next book out. I'll lose the story. Yep, we've all been there and I hear you. I go back to what I said originally.

Take the day off.

Wake Up and Smell the Coffee

Today's exercise involves making a cup of coffee and drinking or at least sipping it. Yes, really. Read on, as there's more to it. I promise, this will help you find your writing mojo. It's not often I promise something. It can get you into all sorts of bother.

FOR THOSE OF you who already drink copious amounts of coffee, you may be thinking, this is a complete waste of time. Firstly, change the blend/strength/type of coffee you use. For those of you who wouldn't touch coffee if it was the only drink available, go with me here. At least make, or order, a cup of coffee. It will be worth it.

So, here's the thing, don't just drink the coffee. Or stare at it as the case may be. Notice everything about it – presentation, colour, amount, the steam rising from it. What do you see? How does the coffee in front of you make you feel? Now smell it. What does it remind you of? Again, how does it make you feel? What are your thoughts? Take a sip. Savour it – taste, sensation, texture. Then swallow, again noticing the flavour, sensation, heat, in fact anything about it.

THIS EXERCISE WILL HELP you in two different ways. Firstly, it enhances observational skills, which will help you strengthen your writing. Secondly, the difference in taste and the new experience will send distinctive signals to your brain telling it today is different. So, smell the coffee and get started.

Make a Difference

CARRYING on from the previous exercise, challenge yourself to do something different. This can be as simple as brushing your teeth with the opposite hand. No, I'm not mad. Or you could take a different route to a favourite café, or take the bus instead of using the car. Again, this changes the signals to the brain telling it that today is different. It will be ready for everything about the day to be turned on its head and will allow your writing mojo to come winging its way back demanding you write. Your creative brain won't have time to think about being on holiday.

Music Madness

MUSIC CAN GET you in the mood, or help you concentrate. Depending on what you choose, of course. If you're writing romance – listen to love songs before you start writing. Sing along to them and really soak up the atmosphere. Writing crime or thriller, crank up the volume and listen to some rock or metal. Once you're in the right frame of mind, change to classical music playing low in the background. This is known to aid concentration and some studies suggest Mozart is particularly suitable for this. Who knew? One caveat – don't let the music last so long you run out of time to write. After all, you need space for the creative side to strut its stuff.

Walk it Out

GET OUT FROM THE HOUSE, out from the office, out from the coffee shop and take a walk. Stride out somewhere different. Make it fast, mixed with a slow meander. Pick your pace up, slow it down. Power walk as fast as you can. This will have your brain wondering what on earth is going on. It will also have several different benefits.

1. Exercise is good for the brain, improving memory and thinking skills. Exactly what a writer needs.
2. As you walk, pay attention to your heart rate,

breathing, how you feel. How do your feet feel on concrete, paving stones, grass or earth? How does it feel walking in rain, wind, snow, sun, cloud, fog? Are you hot? Are you cold? How different do you feel walking slowly, walking fast? Record all this on a digital voice recorder, you'll find you probably have one on your phone. Now, use the details in your stories, giving depth to characters and setting.

3. Take photographs of your surroundings – wide angle, panoramic, close up – as many different shots as you can. What do the paving stones look like - are their cracks, hummocks in the grass, daisies, buttercups, flowers, broken glass, rubbish? Every tiny detail. You can use this in your WIP or future books, allowing you to provide realistic detail. You can also use it to motivate you further down the line.

So, what are you waiting for? Walk it out.

Reach for the Stars

IF YOU LIVE in the city, this one may involve a wee trip to the country. For obvious reasons, this also means in darkness. Get away from the city lights and look at the stars. Really look at the stars. If you're able, lie on a blanket and spend some time gazing at the night sky. Marvel in the vastness of the galaxy. Think of the vastness of the universe. Allow the wonder of the scene to soak into you, the peace to sooth you. Relax and enjoy. Nothing more.

AS YOU DO THIS, thoughts may float into your mind, fleeting

thoughts that can be used in your books. Your unconscious brain will take over. Record these digitally. Take photographs of the sky. Record thoughts, feelings, anything you observe. Savour every single peaceful moment and let the space in your brain be filled with the wonder of space.

3

Release Your Inner Artist

Before you create, do some creating. If you have paints, pens, crayons or pencils in the house go and get them out now. If not, buy some. Keep it simple, keep it cheap – unless you're Van Gogh of course, in which case go for broke. Now, paint, draw or doodle whatever you want. It can be anything. This is not for the Scottish National Gallery or any other gallery for that matter. Draw whatever comes to mind, use different colours, different mediums and above all else, have fun. If your mind is telling you that you're not an artist, tell it to get stuffed. Really hung up on where to start? Then paint or draw colours on the page. Have fun with colour and see where it takes you.

THIS WILL ALLOW you to release a wholly different creative side of your brain. Whilst you are doing it your unconscious mind will continue to work on your story allowing you to come up with fresh ideas. Also, the fact you have put something down on paper will tell your brain it has already started, getting it over that I don't know where to start feeling.

So, what are you waiting for? – off you go. Release your inner Monet.

$\sim$

Make Waves

YES, that's right, waves in real life and brain waves. This one involves a trip to the beach, or a river, or any body of water you can find. Take a notebook, pen and a nice soft towel. Yes, that well-known writers' accessory, a towel. Make sure it's an old one you don't mind using outside. Chop, chop, there's an activity waiting.

TO PARAPHRASE A WELL-KNOWN PHRASE, first find your water. Now you've found some, sit down and observe the water. Watch how it moves. Throw stones in it, look at the effect. Are the waves crashing or lapping gently? Is the river flowing fast or more slowly? Is the pond still, or does it have ripples from a light breeze or a fierce wind? Can you see reflections? Really focus on the water. Let the sights and sound soothe your brain and let the unconscious mind take over.

DIP your hand in the water. Shed shoes and socks and paddle. How does it make you feel? Of course, only do this if it's safe. If your body of water is Niagara Falls you might want to skip those steps.

. . .

SIT ON YOUR TOWEL. Pick up a notebook. Write whatever comes to mind. Thoughts, feelings, descriptions, anything whatsoever. Now you've started writing, transfer it to your WIP. Use that mojo well.

∾

It's all in a Name

TODAY, we're going to have fun with names. Exploring names for characters can bring to mind some interesting brand-new characters or set up a spark of creativity which can turn into a burning fire. There are different ways you can do this.

1. Brainstorm first and second names.
2. Look up popular baby names for the year your character was born.
3. Look up popular names in the country in which your character was born.
4. Visit a cemetery and look at the names on the gravestones. May I suggest you use historical cemeteries rather than using the names of the recently deceased. However, you can mix and match first and second names.
5. Use a name generator app on your phone. I've got one called 'Name Dice' on my iPhone but a quick search shows there are numerous others available.
6. Look through the telephone book or yellow pages.

OF COURSE, if you still remember the name of the little torag who stole your rubber in primary two, now might be the time to use him or her as a not so nice character. Revenge is a dish best served in the pages of a book.

What's in a Word?

NOW YOU'VE HAD fun with names, it's time to turn your attention to words. There are so many words in the world and we use only a fraction of them each day. Now let's be clear here, I'm not suggesting you obfuscate your novel with long and allegedly intelligent words. Whilst using more words is a good thing, especially if you are wont to repeat yourself, clouding the issue isn't. Most readers want to be stretched but not to the extent where they are pulled out of the story every couple of paragraphs working out the meaning of a labyrinthine word as they head for the nearest dictionary. Keep it uncomplicated. Unless, of course, you are writing a Thesaurus, in which case have at it.

FOR TODAY'S exercise grab a sheet of paper and some coloured pens. The larger the paper the better. Flip chart paper is ideal. Jot down random words, then think of other ways of saying them. Write them large, write them small. Find more words from the Thesaurus. Add them. Today, you are simply going to soak yourself in the beauty and wonder of words.

ONCE YOU'VE DONE this for an hour, have a cup of tea or any other drink for that matter. If it's nine in the morning, you might not want to be drinking gin but it's your choice. Relax and think about the words you have just written down. Let them float around in your brain and permeate your being.

Then return to your WIP and start to form them into sentences. That sneaky subconscious will already be creating sentences, ideas and thoughts on ways the story can zoom forwards.

~

A Rose by any Other Name

WAKE UP AND SMELL THE... roses.

OR ANY FLOWERS as long as they smell. Walk around a garden. Take deep breaths and inhale the scents. Let them soothe and relax you. Either pick or buy a bunch of flowers and display them in your office, letting them cheer up the room and fill it with beauty.

THINK of different words that can be used to describe flowers. Take one rose and study it. Write down every single thing about it. Sight, smell, touch. Keep writing. Use it as the basis of a story.

Now, smell the roses and enjoy everything about them.

~

The Beat of a Different Drum

TODAY, you're going to make a wild noise. If you can get access to a drum kit, go truly wild. If not, channel your inner child and use pots, pans and any other implements useful for making a drumming noise. Raise the roof and enjoy every minute. Today, you are going to march to the beat of a different drum. Nothing more – that's it.

Baby, it's Cold Outside

SAVE THIS ONE FOR WINTER. Wrap up and take a walk outside. This will get the blood pumping and fire up your brain. Pay close attention to the way you feel. The wind on your face, the cold on your skin. As you walk, allow the cold to energise you, to fire up your brain. Notice your breathing, your heartbeat, the temperature of your body. Think about a character in your book or story? How would they feel about the weather you are experiencing? Have they ever seen snow before? Is this the norm for them and they pay it no heed? Is the weather foiling their attempt to solve the mystery, save the damsel in distress, reach their child or whatever the hero or heroine's quest is?

IF YOU'RE READING this in a country where the temperature never gets cold enough to put on winter clothes, crank up the air conditioning full blast, close your eyes and imagine you're in the snow. After all, you're someone who makes things up for a living.

4

Feel the Heat

This is the polar (or Sahara) opposite of the previous exercise. Do exactly the same but crank up the heat. Let's see what being warm can do to get those creative juices flowing. What is your brain telling you and how does your character feel? Off you go and look out your summer clothes. Yes, even in Scotland.

Playtime

IF YOU'VE GOT children or grandchildren, spend an hour simply playing with them. Observe how they use their imagination as they play. Let them guide you and lead you as you spend time in their world. Enjoy being a child again. If you don't have children, borrow some from a friend. They will always be happy for you to take the kids off their hands for a couple of hours. Simply immerse yourself in a different world where everything is simpler. Again, this has a twofold result. You'll find yourself relaxing and you'll be able to write realistic children into your WIP.

ONE CAVEAT – Please don't spend time watching random children you don't know. This may lead you to researching the inside of a police cell for real. Definitely not the best way of sparking your creativity.

Make a Game of It

TODAY, you really do need to release your inner child. Imagine a scene from your current work and make it into a game. Act it out and see how it would play out in real life. Go with me here, no matter how weird you feel. Using movement and all your senses will help make the scene come alive. Remember though, it's a game. No real people should be harmed in the execution of this activity.

Fly Away

THERE ARE several ways you can do this activity.

1. If you can, fly somewhere for a short writing retreat.
2. Take the train somewhere for a short writing retreat.
3. Take the bus to a different city and have a one-day writing retreat.

Even if you can drive, take public transport. This will let

your brain know there is something different going on and prepare it for change. Getting away from it all will allow you to concentrate on writing and leave behind all the things your brain usually tells you need to be done as a matter of urgency.

~

Go Bananas

LITERALLY, go bananas. Dance like no one is looking – mainly because no one is. Crank up the music and sing along as loud as you can to your favourite songs. Pretend you are your favourite artist at the O2 or Hollywood Bowl. Release all those excitable endorphins and let them work their magic in your body. Now, I know you might feel a bit daft doing this but, trust me, it will give you more freedom than you will ever know. Your creativity will thank you for it.

~

Word Wise

LET'S have some fun with words. Words are powerful weapons - they can be used to steer your reader in different directions or allow their brains to take them in another direction altogether. Many words sound the same, are said the same or even spelt the same and yet they mean different things. Take the title of this book – *Motivation Matters*. This could mean motivation is important, which is true. It can also mean everything pertaining to motivation, which is also true. You may have consciously taken this in, why not you've paid good money, or this comes as a revelation to you. Trust me, even if you didn't know, your brain will have worked it out.

. . .

So, let's play with words. Think of as many words as you can that sound the same or are the same and have different meanings. This will get your brain fired up and ready to carry on writing.

Right, write right now.

Nature Calls

Spend the day in the countryside, park, Nature Park, wildlife centre or anywhere you can commune with nature. Enjoy, take in the sights and refresh yourself.

5

The World Around Us

Today is given over to looking at the world around you. Spend an hour looking at every aspect of your surroundings - colour, depth, texture, activity, people, clothing, smell, and sound. Make a concerted effort to use all your senses. Listen to what people are saying. Touch the walls, the grass, the buildings. Have a drink and pay attention to the taste. Feel the slap of your feet on the stones or the soft grass under your feet. How do your clothes feel as they touch your skin?

Now use this heightened awareness and start writing. Write now.

~

Chit Chat

TAKE yourself off to a café for an hour. Listen to the conversation around you. Write down thoughts, sayings and ideas you can use in your books. I'm not saying write things down verbatim but take in the way people speak. The mannerisms they use, the ebb and flow of conversation. Use this as the basis of realistic dialogue in your book.

WHILE YOU ARE AT IT, have a nice cup of coffee and a slice of cake, and enjoy. Writing books can be so much fun.

Idle Dreams

SPEND the first half hour of the day letting your mind take you where it will. Think of your hopes and dreams and where you would like to be as an author. What do you want to achieve? What is important to you?

Now, write this down and use it as the basis to set goals. Your writing can suffer if you don't know why you are doing it, or where you want it to take you. Change that today and then start writing.

MY GOAL IS to make £100,000 per year from my writing and that certainly keeps me motivated. What are your goals?

Forget About It

TODAY IS A DAY OFF. Forget about everything and enjoy life. You are so much more than a writer. You are you and it's important to look after yourself. So, spend today doing what you enjoy the most. Your writing will thank you for it. Off you go, there's fun to be had. Now, if you'll excuse me, I'm off to build sandcastles on the beach.

∼

Let it Slip

OFTEN, one of the reasons you can't get motivated is because you think you have writer's block. Let me explain, you may be struggling with the chapter you are writing at the moment rather than suffering from writer's block So, slip forward in time and write a different chapter. Trust me, your subconscious will be taking over and thinking about the original chapter as well. The subconscious is a tenacious wee thing and isn't going to give up easily. You'll find it will deliver the right direction to you, all wrapped up nicely with a bonnie wee bow. Now is the time to make a change for a change.

∼

We Like to Move It.

AS THE SONG GOES, We Like to Move It. And today you are going to make movement your friend and allow it to help channel your writing mojo. First things first, put down the pen, step away from the keyboard. Now find your phone or preferably a digital voice recorder. Phone means distraction, DVR means stepping away from all communication. Today you will be dictating your writing as you go for a walk – around the neigh-bourhood, in the park, in the woods, around the house, up and down the stairs – whatever gets your pulse up a bit. Exercise gets the brain working faster and, in a two for one deal, makes you fitter. Motivation and fitness – you can't say you don't get value added in this book.

Location, Location, Location

IT'S time to change the place you write. Now, if you're writing up a storm in your usual place, with a cup of tea and a nice custard cream, then keep going. However, if that's the case I guess you wouldn't be using this book. So, on your feet and take yourself somewhere else to write. Move from your office/study to the dining room or kitchen table. Go to a library or a coffee shop. Heck if the sun's shining, write on a park bench or the botanical gardens. Not literally on the park bench of course. Oh, you know what I mean.

WHEREVER YOU GO MAKE it somewhere you've never written before. If you'll excuse me I'm off to the café in my local garden centre. I might even come home with a few tomato plants.

_____

6

It's all Chinese to Me

This one is about having fun with words. Use an online translator to translate your work into seven different languages and see what it looks like to others. It's also about dreaming and aiming high. Imagine how you would feel if the books were really available in those languages. Picture yourself in Paris, Amsterdam, Beijing or any other capital city looking at your book front and foremost in a bookshop window. Now, let your writing take you there. Anything is possible.

Dance Moves

FIND A DANCE MIX, switch the music on, crank up the volume and dance like the world is going to end. This will get the blood pumping, fire up your brain and get you ready to face anything. No set time – 5 minutes, 10 minutes, 30 minutes – you're in charge. Your brain will be pumped up and firing on every neurone. Channel this new found energy into your writing and give it a different vibe. Write as fast as you can, keeping the energy going and watch that word count soar.

∼

And Relax

AFTER YESTERDAY'S frenetic activity you're going to turn it completely on its head today. Find a space where you will be comfortable and lie down. Steady your breathing. Take a breath in for the count of six, hold for the count of seven, out for the count of eight. As you relax, let your subconscious take over and form plots, ideas and schemes in your head. As they rise to the surface, change these with each breath. Let them take a more solid form as the story takes place in front of your very eyes. Do this for ten minutes then get up and write them down. That's you started writing for the day so, keep the momentum going.

∼

Boxed In

TAKE one large sheet of flipchart paper. Draw four large boxes, each in a different colour. Head the boxes – People, Places, Purpose, Plot.

Now, fill these boxes with any random thoughts about each of the titles. No matter how inconsequential it may seem, write it down. Your brain will begin to form links and firm ideas of where the storyline should go. It will help to strengthen characters and setting and lead to your characters heading in different directions in order to fulfil their purpose. Now you're ready to write all those exciting new ideas into your story. Who knows, it might even lead you in an entirely different, yet exciting, new direction – one leading to a brand new novel.

Oranges and Lemons

No, nothing to do with the Bells of St Clements. However, the zingy, sharp smell of citrus can give your brain some extra zing. Cut into fruit such as oranges, lemons and limes, and breath in the scent of each. Now make lemonade. You know the saying, when life gives you lemons, make lemonade, and why waste the fruit. Drink the citrus concoction and then write. I can guarantee, your brain will be sitting up and begging to get on with it.

A Different Beat

OPEN UP whatever music app you use or crack out your CDs or vinyl collection. Now, listen to four or five different tracks, all of which have a different beat. Write down ideas and notes as you listen and allow the music to direct your writing. Don't stop to think about it or edit, just write as fast as you can.

ONCE YOU'VE FINISHED READ back over what you've written. Did your writing style change with the music change? If so, how did it change? Use this to develop the uniqueness of your characters. Dare to be different and see where it leads.

Moving On

TODAY'S EXERCISE is for those who feel writers' block has really struck, or for those who are suffering from a saggy middle. Don't you just hate it when your middle sags? Despite the title, this is not an exercise regime but a literal moving on. Simply put the current part of your whip aside and move on to a different part. While you are concentrating on scenes further in the book your clever old (or young) brain will be working out all the links. Let it strut its stuff and come back to the sagging scene later.

7

Unchained Melody

Following on from the 'Different Beat' exercise imagine your character in each of the songs you listened to. If you're dipping in and out of the exercises, it's better to do Different Beat before this one. How would he or she react? How would this change them? What would they do in response to what is happening? Use this new found knowledge to give this character more depth and breadth.

Moving Further

CHOOSE YET another part of your book and work on it today. Your brain will come up with endless possibilities of where situations can change or go in your WIP. These are deliberately close together in order to allow your brain to make connections. The few days part is to give your brain time to work out anything complex. Let your brain have at it and it will do you proud.

Fill in the Blanks

THIS IS another exercise designed to help your brain make connections. This one involves drawing a mind map. I've even left a space at the end of the chapter ready for your mind map. Use coloured pens and write down all the plot points you already have. Leave gaps in the lines where you feel you are stuck. Take another sheet of paper and jot down ideas for your WIP. Then fill in the blanks on this mind-map. You'll find you have some eureka moments in the process.

Up a Tree

I DON'T LITERALLY WANT you to go up a tree for this one. Unless you fancy it of course, or have a tree house, then feel free. This is linked to the hero's quest. The saying goes, put your hero up a tree and then throw stones at them. This is an analogy for putting obstacles in their way. Grab a large sheet of paper and write down all the different obstacles you can think of in order to stop your protagonist reaching their goal. This can be anything. Be as inventive as you like. Once you've done this, choose three to use. There you go. No longer stuck but with fresh ideas to get you writing like a banshee. Ooh, I wonder if a banshee could be an obstacle for my character. Now there's a thought.

The Sound of Silence

TAKE yourself to a place where there is complete silence. Lie down and absorb that silence for an hour. Concentrate on relaxing and listening to your own heartbeat. You will be amazed at how much noise there is in the modern world, no matter where you go. The silence will give your brain a rest and allow it to clear itself. You'll be amazed at how quickly it will start to work on a storyline and untangle any knotty problems.

Sand Castles

YES, that's right, you're off to build sandcastles. Buy yourself a bucket and spade, and some little cardboard flags you can write on. Go to the beach, borrow a neighbour's sand pit, or go to a playpark (preferably one with no children using it) where there is a sandpit. Spend half an hour building the most magnificent and complex sandcastle you can imagine. As you do, imagine each individual part of the castle is a part of your WIP. As an idea comes to you write it on a flag and stick it in a rampart or a wall. Or the centre, or the gate. You get the picture – wherever you think it fits best. Now take a photo or draw the castle in a notebook. Make sure you can see where the flags are.

THIS CASTLE IS a physical personal mind map. The fact you are using sight, hearing, touch, smell, and physical exercise will give your brain that extra edge. The more senses you use, the more your brain will take in. Plus, it's great fun. What are you waiting for?

Little Sips

GRAB YOUR FAVOURITE DRINK. Rather than gulping it down in a hurried rush, take the time to savour every tiny sip. If you savour the flavour and absorb the texture and temperature it will give your brain time to slow down and catch up. Give yourself and your brain a break.

8

Put Down the Phone

T his may be a scary thought for some but that's what makes it even more important. Today you are going to spend the entire day without touching a mobile phone. Leave it in another room and do not touch it, not once, until you have finished writing for the day. You may feel like you've cut off your arm or go through withdrawal symptoms but, trust me, you will cope. Your brain will thank you for it when it has all that extra time to write.

Writing Prompt

USE the following words in your WIP or as the basis for a short story or poem.

UNDERSTAND - Briefs - Complimentary - Chocolate - Buzzard

Mood Massage

THERE ARE TWO OPTIONS HERE:

1. Book yourself in for a relaxing massage.
2. Buy some peppermint essential oil and massage into your hands and feet. This can increase alertness and improve concentration.

Heck, if you feel like it, go for broke and do both.

Something New

SPEND time today doing something you've never done before. It doesn't matter what, only you know what fits the bill. If it was me, I might go and do some sketching by the river or read a science fiction book. This will stretch your imagination and stretch you as a person. It will also allow the brain to work in different ways and think of new opportunities.

Word Pairs

GRAB your notebook and start a list of synonyms you can use to change the words you overuse. Start with two synonyms for twenty overused words and keep them safe. Add to these as you go along and build up a nice bank of words. Take them out and read them every couple of days. Your brain will assimilate them and will start to use them naturally as you write.

~

An Exercise Just for You

THINK of a holiday you couldn't stop raving about, or an event you attended that exceeded expectations, or any event that filled you with joy and wonder. Close your eyes and imagine every wondrous detail. Let those happy endorphins flood your body, then start writing. Notice how this revolutionises your prose, how your word count soars and how much you are enjoying the process.

~

Phone a friend

THAT'S all today's exercise is about. Or is it? You should know by now this book always shows two sides of the literary coin. You can phone a friend for a chat and a catch up. Or you can phone a writing chum to discuss a tricky part of your WIP or brainstorm ideas for moving forward. Take notes as you chat. Guess what – you've already started writing, so simply carry on. Genius.

9

Scream and Shout

Before you think I'm getting you to start some sort of wild rant, that aint the case. Of course, you can scream about the unfairness of your writing life, who am I to tell you what to do. However, the jury is out on how much use this will be. It will release adrenaline which speeds up your heartbeat and you might be able to transfer this into writing a scene in which anger is appropriate. On the other hand, you could wander around the office shouting out appropriate words and phrases that will move your WIP forward. The change in tone and voice level will stimulate your brain and get it thinking in a different way.

Highland Fling

No, you don't have to do a Highland Fling but you can if you want. Nor do you need to visit the Highlands of Scotland, although I would highly recommend it. This is about finding the highest spot in your locality and writing about it. Take photos of it. Study it in depth and work out a plotline taking your characters there. It can be done, I promise you. I'm a crime writer, so I also look for spots to dump a body. If you live in the South East of England, which is notoriously flat, the highest point is supposedly Chrishall Common near the village of Langley, at 147m. Who says you don't learn things in this book?

A Nice Cup of Tea

SIT down with a nice cup of tea (other beverages are available) and relax. That's it. Give your body and mind time to calm down. Yes, I know you're busy, now off you go and make a cup of tea. The next thirty minutes are yours.

Silliness of Course

LITERALLY, do something silly. Something you would never think of doing ordinarily. The sky's the limit, in a metaphorical sense, unless flying to Paris for the day is your idea of silliness. In that case, can I join you? I find having fun with hats is both silly and allows me to take on different personas and think. I have the following hats in my house – Army Major (I was in the Army), Sherlock Holmes Cap, Jack the Ripper Top Hat, Hercule Poirot Bowler, Arabic Sheikh, sun hat and a fur hat with Winnie the Pooh on it. Each of these allows my brain to switch course and come up with new ideas. That's one example – do whatever you find is silly and let your brain switch gears. Now if you'll excuse me, I've a hat to find.

∼

Writing Prompt

YOUR CHARACTER IS SITTING in a café and hears the couple behind him (or her) discussing a state secret. Immediately he reaches for ...

∼

You're Having a Giraffe

STOP! No need to run to the zoo. This is one of the cockney rhyming slang phrases for laugh. It's time to do some laughing. Find a video on YouTube that makes you laugh. Watch two or three of these. What is it about them that inspires laughter? Watch the way lines are delivered, what the characters are doing, facial expressions, the nuances of language, the words used, the scenery and setting. Analyse which of these you find the funniest. Then work out how you can use this new found knowledge in your WIP or a short story.

∼

It's Time for Time

YOU'D THINK this would be about taking time for yourself but no, I need to be contrary. This is about using time wisely. Every little, teensy weeny bit of your precious time wisely. Today, pledge to write in every free moment of the day. Waiting for a Dr's appointment? Write in a notebook. Waiting for the kids to come out of school? Write on a phone app. Waiting for dinner to cook? Write on a scrap of paper. Can't sleep? Write in a notebook you keep by the bed especially for this occasion.

After 24 hours, work out how many words you've written. You'll be amazed.

10

Jump to It

Literally, jump to it. Go back to your childhood and do some jumping. If you have a skipping rope (or can nick one from the nearest child) use that to do some jumping. Otherwise, jump up and down on the spot or jump over a low wall. Repeat this several times and get the blood pumping faster around your body. Get some blood and more oxygen to your brain and give it all the energy it needs to be creative.

ONE CAVEAT; broken bones are not good for creativity, so be careful. No actual humans should be harmed in the performing of this exercise.

YOU MIGHT WANT to have a little sit down after this one – resist. Strongly. Straight to your WIP and use all that new found energy to move this glorious manuscript forward. You can always rest later and you'll be glad you carried on. If you really must rest, draw a little mind map below so you know where you are going next with your work.

A Brick Wall

THIS IS all about smashing both a physical brick wall and the brick wall stopping you from writing. Before you get all excitable and smash your way through the garden wall, you first need to build a nice big wall – from Lego Bricks. What, I hear you say? Yep, that's right Lego Bricks. Go find some. Most libraries have them.

NOW YOUR WALL is built you are going to use visualisation. As you smash this newly built wall to pieces, imagine a wall stopping you moving forward in your WIP and smash it to pieces visually. Now is the perfect time to step through the rubble and write, write, write.

Movie Magic

SPEND ten minutes playing a movie in your mind about your WIP and where it is going. You'll find the moving pictures will wake up your creativity and allow it to take you further than you ever imagined before you started. Play the movie over in your head several times.

Reading, not Writing

Iᴛ's time to do some reading, not strictly for pleasure but for research. Choose ten books, from your bookshelves or the library. Unless you fancy buying some new books. Choose different genres and different authors. Now take a chapter from each of them in order to read and analyse them. You may want to photocopy the relevant chapters so you can underline or highlight but it's not necessary. Look at the lengths of the chapters, the language they use, the length of sentences, dialogue, the ebb and flow of the narrative everything about it. How do different genres handle these? Are you able to use any of this research to develop your own writing style and to move your WIP forward?

Genre Switch

I'ᴍ ɴᴏᴛ sᴜɢɢᴇsᴛɪɴɢ you do this for your current manuscript. However, based on yesterday's reading, write a one-hundred-word flash fiction piece in three different genres outside of your usual genre. Step outside your comfort zone and stretch your creative brain. Here's a first sentence to get you started.

You don't often see a leopard roaming the streets of...

Look to the Past

Lᴏᴏᴋ through the historical archives or newspapers at the local library or online. Use these for ideas for a short story or a subplot in your WIP. You can also do this to research popular names from a specific period in history. You'll also have fun to boot, so it's a win whichever way you look at it.

Throwing Stones

IF YOU'RE in an area where there is no one else around, then literally throw stones anywhere, without breaking anything of course. Watch the stones as they fly through the air and let your thoughts follow the trajectory of the stone. As the stone lands, let your mind clarify these thoughts and come up with a solution for any knotty issues in your manuscript. You can also do this by throwing stones into a lake, river or the sea and watching the ripples. Let your thoughts fan out like the ripples and let your mind work out where they are going.

11

Write it Out

Write down all the things that are frustrating you about your current WIP. Now write down all the things you love about it. Every little thing, no matter how inconsequential it seems to you. You'll find, now you're writing, your writer's block will have disappeared in a vortex of words which can be used to shape the next few lines, paragraphs, chapters and pages of your book. Have fun.

Encouragement is Good

SOMETIMES YOU MIGHT FIND yourself telling your brain, "I can't write." Whilst a little self-doubt is normal, too much can paralyse you. Encourage yourself and find encouragement from others. Read out a chapter of your work to others or let them read it. Ask for constructive criticism. You will find the positive comments far outweigh the areas for improvement and you might also find it helps you see how you can quickly and easily move forward.

~

Family First

SPEND the day with your family and put them first. Forget about your writing and spend the day being you, the person. Sometimes other things are more important and once you spend time on these, you will return with your creative reservoir full to overflowing.

~

Explore and Seek

FIND AN AREA OF YOUR CITY, town or village that you've never been to before. Spend the day exploring and looking for hidden wonders. You can even do this in an area with which you think you are familiar. Look up. Look down. Look around.

I DID this in my city and found dates carved above doorways, towers, cupolas, and plaques to people I'd never heard of. I learned more about the history of my town in one day exploring than I had in all the time I lived here. Use this new found knowledge to develop the setting in your writing.

~

Geography Matters

IF YOU ARE WRITING about a real setting, take time to explore it well. The best idea is to go there and see for yourself. However, if you live in the UK and you're writing about the Australian Outback it may be a bit of a leap. Physically at least but metaphorically, in this technological era, you're cooking on gas. Use every online tool possible for research. Contact locals and ask for advice and their take on the area. Spend time soaking up the culture. On the other hand, if you fancy a wee trip now is the time to book your train ticket.

Take a Trip

THIS ONE IS a bit closer to home. Take a trip to the closest, village, town or city where your book is set. Explore it well and see how your main character and the plot could fit in here. You'll find the change of scene will give you lots of new ideas. Plus, you'll feel like you've had a break and come back to writing refreshed.

Look to the Children

YES, I know this is another post about children. I want you to spend the day watching your own, or a borrowed relative's, children. Look at their mannerisms. Listen to their speech. Watch how they move, how they smile, how they interact. In fact, everything about them. Not only will you be able to use snippets of this to make the children in your books more realistic, you will have fun in the process. Please don't watch random children as I don't want to be responsible for your arrest.

12

Calm Down

When you find yourself stuck in a writing sense, very often it can be because life is stressing you out. It's time to slow down and calm down. Use your phone or any other device capable of accessing the Internet and play calming music. I asked Alexa to play calming music and she (it) came up with Classical Music for a Relaxing Bath. I'm not advocating this one, although the title does appeal to me, merely giving an idea of how I found some music. While it is playing, lie down (it doesn't need to be in the bath) and let it soothe you.

∼

Speed it up

YESTERDAY'S EXERCISE was designed to calm you down. Today's is the exact opposite. Let's get the heartbeat pumping with music designed to energise. Now, speed up your writing by doing five-minute sprints. After five minutes, walk around the room for one minute. Now repeat. After ten five-minute word sprints, you'll find you've written more words than you can ever imagine. The most I've done is 3500 words. In fifty minutes. It is possible.

~

There's a Podcast for That

GO TO STITCHER, iTunes or any other Podcast app. Do a search for a writing and/or marketing podcast. Subscribe to this and listen to some of the back episodes. The regular ones I listen to are The Creative Penn, The Sell More Books Show, and Ask ALLi. Listen to some of the back episodes and get yourself motivated to write.

~

The Eyes of a Child

NO, I'm not obsessed with children. This is about seeing things from a different perspective. Get down to the height of a child and look around you. How different does the world look? Are you noticing more than you would usually? Use this newly found insight in your writing.

~

Release Your Inner David Bailey

CARRYING on from yesterday's exercise this is also about seeing things from a different perspective. Take your camera out and about. This can be a phone camera or the highest end DSLR. It doesn't really matter. It's about looking at things up close and in wide angle. Snap photos of the world around you, getting in close and standing right back. When you get home, look at them on a wide screen or print them out. Examine them carefully and take in all the detail. Can you now see things you missed when looking with the naked eye?

They're All Dead

TAKE yourself off to an ancient cemetery and spend time communing with the dead. Actually, that's a joke, you're not going to be communing with anyone. However, take a look at the gravestones and from the details on them write a short story, a piece of flash fiction, or a couple of paragraphs for your novel. There's nothing like an old gravestone to conjure up images in your head. Of course, if you're a crime writer, these images may involve more death but who am I to judge.

Move Over

LITERALLY, move over. To the other side of the room. Change your seat, change your desk, change your view and change your outlook. Your brain will start to see things in new ways and this will help you to get writing again. A simple one today.

13

Tell Someone Else

One of the ways you can overcome the fact you're stuck is to talk it over with someone else. Use a close friend or a writing group or even the dog. However, if they are human, they can respond and that helps. Speaking it out loud might be just what's needed for your brain to make the right connections. On the other hand, your friend might say something that provides the missing link in your story. What have you got to lose? Especially if the chat involves coffee and cake? Bonus.

Libraries Matter

THIS WAS a recent campaign aimed at keeping libraries in the UK open. I can assure you they certainly do matter, especially to you today. Visit your local library, tell the librarian what you are stuck with, and trust me she or he will recommend the perfect book to help you. If you're writing up a storm, just borrow a book from the library and spend time reading.

Go Green

THIS IS NOT about saving the planet, although that is admirable, it's about spotting the colour green. What, I hear you say? Why bother? Why indeed. On a recent car journey, I switched off the music and turned on my vision, making a concerted effort to look for the colour green. Now, what sounds better?

ON HER WAY TO ABERDEEN, Cass rode past a lorry.

On her way to Aberdeen, Cass passed an Eastern European lorry, a bright green dragon snaking over the doorway and down the side. She spent the rest of the journey pondering the significance of the dragon

YES, I really did see that.

Here's One I Made Earlier

GO BACK to a previous story or novel not yet completed. Let your mind work on it for the next couple of hours. Take a break and go back to your original WIP. Changing tack gives your brain the kickstart it needs.

Puddles of Fun

FOR OBVIOUS REASONS you need rain for this one. Put on your wellies and spend some time splashing about in puddles. Note how it makes you feel. If it merely makes you feel miserable then at least you can channel that feeling into your writing when a character is walking about in the rain.

IF YOU'RE in the middle of a heatwave when you read this, either wait for a rainy day or fill up a paddling pool in the back garden and paddle about in your bare feet. Remember, do something different and your brain will quickly catch on.

Do you Know Your Left from Your Right?

THAT'S a rhetorical question as I'm sure you do. This exercise is simple – or extremely difficult, depending on how you look at it. Grab a notebook and pen. Hold the pen in your non-dominant hand and write out two paragraphs of your current work. Your brain will be so busy concentrating on the task being hard that all thoughts of writers' block will fly out of the window.

Listen to Me

OR RATHER LISTEN to everyone else. Go for a walk along a busy street. Spend some time in a crowded tourist attraction. Sit in a Café. Whatever idea floats your boat. Make a concerted effort to listen to those around you. Use these snippets of conversation as:

1. An idea for a book.
2. A plot twist.
3. Dialogue ideas – not the conversation in its entirety but as a means of making dialogue realistic.

14

More Books Than You Know

Visit a library and browse the shelves. Pull one book, from seven different genres. Read a random chapter from each of the books. Or chapter seven from each of them if you prefer. Study the different writing styles. How do they set the tone? How does the author give an idea of setting? What words are used? Your brain will soak up information like a sponge and use it to spark renewed creativity.

A Novel Idea

BREAK OUT of the cycle of staring at a blank screen by picking up a paper and pen. Now jot down twenty ideas for future novels. Yes, you heard right. Twenty. Once you've done that, write one sentence about each of them. Now you are writing use this new found creativity - back to your WIP and start writing. As an added bonus, you've started twenty new books. That should keep you busy for some time.

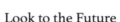

Look to the Future

SPEND thirty minutes thinking about what your characters may be doing 1, 5, 10 years in the future. Jot down notes as you go. How might knowing this shape the person they are today. Write down every idea that comes to you, no matter how inconsequential it might seem. This might be the idea that makes the difference to a decision your character might make, or how they react. Also, having notes available to cut and paste into your work can help you when you feel you need something to get you unstuck.

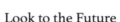

Why do I do That

WHY INDEED? How often do you think about the decisions you make or the actions you take? I know I often do things by pure gut instinct. Or is that the case? Often gut instinct is governed by your past, decisions you have made previously and experience. How often do you analyse a characters' motivation, decision making and actions they take? Analysis can help you to understand your character more fully and make them a more rounded personality.

WHAT A CHARACTER THEY WILL BE.

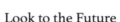

Where in the World?

HAVE you thought about taking your main character on a trip abroad? Yes, I know the elderly character in your cozy mystery only struts their stuff in one village. Think of the endless possibilities that could open up if you send them on a world cruise. What have you got to lose?

~

Look at it from Another Point of View

LOOKING at the scene from the point of view of a different character can open up insights into how it could or should unfold. Step out of the head of your main character and into the head of one of the others. I'm not suggesting you head hop, just do this as an exercise to see if it makes a difference and gets you past a sticky patch. This exercise is particularly good for saggy middles.

~

The Sun and the Sky

PLEASE DO NOT STARE at the sun for this exercise as I don't want to be responsible for any eye problems. However, do look at the sky and take in the beauty. Let it relax you and feel the warm sun on your face. This exercise is all about relaxing and feeling peaceful. The sun usually makes you feel a lot better about everything, including your writing.

PART two of this is to go outside and write. A change of place always makes the writing flow more smoothly.

15

Step away from the Computer

Put down your notebook and pen. It's time for another break to fill the empty creative reservoir. Do whatever will help *you* creatively. Exercise? Go for it. Art Gallery, day trip, museum, reading, swimming, day at the beach? The sky's your limit. The day is yours, so enjoy every minute.

Writing Prompt

A MAN with a prosthetic leg is seen climbing in a window.

Water, Water Everywhere

THIS IS about drinking more during the day. Dehydration fogs the brain and stifles creativity. Starting with a nice cup of tea really is a good plan. As is keeping a bottle of water nearby. Plan frequent drink stops throughout the day.

It's All Around Us

INSPIRATION THAT IS. As you go about your normal daily routine, look for inspiration and ideas for your book or for a short story or poem. There's even white space at the end of the chapter for you to jot some ideas down.

Writing Prompt

CARRYING on from yesterday's theme of water.

AS THE WATER ROSE HIGHER, she...

Can You Feel It?

THERE ARE two strands to today's creative exercise:

1. Do something you've never done before. Something that takes you out of your comfort zone. Pay close attention to your feelings and write them down.
2. You are going to use touch to explore the world. As you go about your daily routine and are out and about, close your eyes and explore objects using only touch. This will heighten your senses and give

you a new outlook. Yes, the world might think you are mad – explain you're an author and they will nod their heads and move on.

Touch Box

We're taking yesterday's exercise on touch a stage further. Ask a friend to make you up a box with different objects in it. The box must be sealed and have only openings for your hands. No peeking. Try to work out what the objects are. Again, you will get a different appreciation of an object by using a different sense.

16

The Other Side of the Street

This is about viewing your surroundings from a different angle. If you are anything like me, you will be a creature of habit. If you are walking from A to B on a familiar route you will travel the same way every time. Literally, cross the street and see how much more you take in. The very act of making a change will make you look more closely, rather than daydreaming.

IF YOU ARE SOMEWHERE new walk the same route twice, using a different side of the street each time. What do you see differently?

THIS CAN BE USED EFFECTIVELY to wake your brain up and let it know things are different now.

∽

Far, Far Away

TRANSPORT your main character to the other side of the world. From my home in Scotland, I'm reliably informed this is Australia for me. Spend the next hour thinking about how they would react and deal with the unfamiliar surroundings, characters and culture. Use this newfound insight into your character's psyche to shape the next decision they make.

ON THE OTHER HAND, my character would probably be too busy noshing on barbecue to make any decent decision. Note to self - make sure there's no food around.

Third star to the Left

No, not the boy who never grew up – he talked about a star to the right. This is about using your imagination in a 'the sky's the limit' sort of way. Dream big dreams about your books and you as an author. Now write down three goals. One short term, one mid-term and one long term.

1.

2.

3.

Animal Magic

INCORPORATE AN ANIMAL INTO YOUR WIP, the more outrageous the better. In my crime books, I have had lambs roaming around the police station, a Weimaraner puppy with behavioural issues, a cat who changes gender and the thickest Bernese Mountain Dog you have ever met. It keeps the characters on their toes and allows you to develop humorous subplots.

∾

Raindrops Keep Falling

NOT ON YOUR head but your characters' heads. Not just a few raindrops but a deluge. I'm talking monsoon levels of rain here. The type that floods cities and makes rivers burst their banks. Now, provide your characters with a compelling or inescapable reason to go out in this. How do they cope? What is their reaction? How does it hamper their ability to get the job done? How do they overcome obstacles? How do they react? How do they feel? Does it strengthen their resolve or weaken them? Do they demonstrate leadership skills or turn into Moaning Minnies?

∾

Every Grain of Sand...

IS THERE FOR A REASON. Sometimes that reason is for fun, another time it's to hamper. Close your eyes and imagine you are in quicksand. It is slowly pulling you in and you need help. How do you feel? What do you do? What is happening to your heart rate? What thoughts go through your mind.

NOW THAT YOU'VE frightened yourself to death, put a character in a perilous situation and use your feelings to shape how the character would react and the actions they would take.

Release Your Inner Child

GO TO THE LIBRARY. Borrow three children's picture books. Read them one after the other. What do they have in common with regards to the plot? What can the simplicity of this teach you about plotting your own book? How can you use the techniques to help your own writing journey? Oh, and don't forget to simply enjoy the stories.

17

Run, Run as Fast as You Can

This really is about going out for a run. If your last run was in the hundred-yard dash at primary school, then maybe take it slowly to start with as I don't want to be responsible for anyone collapsing. If you can't run, then go for a brisk walk. Get your heart rate up and the blood pumping especially to the brain. You will think more clearly and it will enhance creativity. Off you go and find those running shoes.

Are we there yet?

This one is simple. Look back on how far you've come in the book you are writing.
Seriously, you can rock this writing lark.
If it's the start of a brand new book, look back on how far you've come in your journey.

Seriously, you can rock this writing lark.
If you're staring at the first page of your first ever book, look
back over how far you've come in life.
Seriously, you can rock this writing lark.

∾

And Breathe

Lie, or sit, somewhere quiet. Close your eyes and concentrate
on breathing. In to the count of six, hold for seven, out to the
count of eight. Do this for ten minutes and feel yourself relax.
When you are finished. Start writing.

∾

There's an App for That

THERE ARE numerous writing apps out in the electronic
universe, all of which will help you with your writing or organi-
sation. My two favourites are *Evernote*, which syncs over all my
devices, and *Lists for Authors*. I use *Evernote* for note keeping,
writing on the go, photographs and articles all stored in files for
each WIP.

HAVE a look in the App store and see what you can find.

∾

This Little Teddy Went to Market

TAKE a Teddy out and about with you today. See how many
conversations you can strike up and how much fun it can be.

What's that, you feel a bit daft. I refer you back to what I said at the beginning of the book, these exercises are an opportunity to blow yourself out of your comfort zone. Your creative brain will thank you for it. Plus, the teddy can help you write the book.

~

Let Them Eat Cake

OR RATHER, let yourself eat cake. Okay, you might be doing this at 7am and even I agree that's too early for cake. You've got permission to do this later in that case. Use the cake to motivate you for a writing goal. Once you've written the correct amount of words or for a certain length of time, sit down with a nice drink and slice of cake. Enjoy every morsel. This is about pampering yourself. If you don't like cake, feel free to substitute. Other treats are available.

~

Born Free

TODAY IS a free day for you to do exactly what you want. Within the boundaries of the law of course, as I'm not coming to bail you out and this book cannot be used as a defence argument. Enjoy your day.

18

To the Moon and Back

Don a space suit. Only joking. This exercise takes place over several different nights. Look at the moon in all its phases using the same location each time. Take in your surroundings. How does the sky change it? How can you use this newfound knowledge in your WIP?

Time for Tennis

FIND a partner and have a game of tennis. Not got a partner, do what you did as a child and hit the ball against the wall. Preferably your own wall, or childhood memories really will come back to haunt you. Remember, the very act of doing something different will give your brain a kick up the neurones. If you already play tennis twice a week, use your non-dominant hand. If you're already an expert at that, have a day off, genius.

~

Awareness

As you walk around today, make a concerted effort to take in everything around you. If you are at home, do the same. You will find there is a lot more to see than you usually take in. The problem with doing this at home is -

If you'll excuse me I'm off to grab a mop and some polish.

~

Make a Change for a Change

Do something wildly different. Changing what you do will change the way you think. For example, make every single piece of clothing you are wearing a different colour. Yes, even different coloured socks. Your brain will wonder what the heck is going on and will be all over the place. If the idea of this fills you with horror, tell your critical self you will wear something less jarring once you've written a thousand words. You'll be amazed at how quickly this happens. I can't wait to see what ideas you come up with.

~

Daydreams

Give your brain permission to daydream. Sit somewhere pleasant, with a nice outlook and let your mind have at it. Do this for half an hour. Use one thing you thought of to start the next part of your WIP. Look at that, you're writing up a storm.

~

Try Something New

THINK of something you've always wanted to do but never done before. If this is to backpack around the world leading the laptop lifestyle, you might want to plan that rather than starting right now. Start with something doable. If you are backpacking around the world, don't forget your copy of this book.

NOW, where did I put that backpack?

~

Dear Diary

START A WRITING DIARY. Write down how you are feeling about your writing, the number of words you write in a day, and any general ideas. This can be used as motivation when you don't know where to go in the future.

19

Writing Prompt

Use the following four words in the next paragraph of your work in progress -

Nine - Necessary - Flame - Help

If it's a children's picture book then use these words -

Lost - Jam - Reason - Bumble Bee

Have fun with words.

~

Seeing Red

WATCH out for the colour red today. I noticed a post box, robin, a kilt (I'm Scottish, it's inevitable), pen, water bottle, butterfly on the side of a tissue box and many other things too numerous to mention. I certainly took in a lot more than I usually do and you can too.

~

The Great Artists

PART 1 -TAKE a trip to the nearest art gallery. Look at the paintings by the great artists or even lesser known artists. What is it about these paintings that make them worthy of so much attention? Analyse the depth and layers and attention to detail. Then use aspects of this in your work. However, remember to spend time enjoying the paintings for their own sake.

PART 2 – take a notebook or laptop with you and spend time writing in the café of the art gallery. Use the information while it's fresh in your mind. Writing somewhere new will also tell your brain things are different.

~

Time for a Laugh

FIND a book that is guaranteed to make you laugh. For me, it's any book by Janet Evanovich. Or may I suggest my own *Cass Claymore Investigates* – the first in the series is *Antiques and Alibis*. Simply spend the day reading and having a laugh.

A Grand Day Out

ANOTHER BREAK DAY. Have a day out. Refresh and recharge your batteries. If anything comes along that you think would make good fodder for a book, quickly jot it down and go back to having fun. Enjoy your day off.

An Eggstra Special Day

HAVE some form of egg for breakfast – fried, scrambled, coddled, poached, boiled – whatever you fancy. Eggs are packed full of nutrients needed for brain health. Give your brain a helping hand.

IF YOU ARE allergic to eggs then, in the name of all that's sensible, stay away from this one. In other news, smoked salmon is also good for brain health.

IF YOU'RE VEGAN, nuts, seeds, avocado's and tomatoes are also good for brain health. You're welcome.

Mood Music

Yep, we've done this one before but here's the kicker. You are going to use music differently. Switch the genres around.

If you're writing crime, listen to some romantic music.

If you're writing romance, get into some rock music.

If you're writing fantasy, listen to classical music, it's out of this world. Groan.

Give your neurones a good old healthy kick up the synapses.

20

Savour Every Moment

For the next hour do the following.

1. Set a timer for 5 minutes and write as fast as you can. No thinking - just write.
2. Step away from the computer and relax for 5 minutes. Savour the peace.
3. Rinse and repeat until the hour is up.

How many words did you write? How did the downtime help you? I can bet my pension that in the down time your brain was coming up with fresh ideas.

∼

Well Hydrated

I've recently bought a water bottle that holds 750 mls of water. It is marked off with times throughout the morning and afternoon. This is the recommended amount of water you should drink every hour. Set a timer and drink a glass of water every hour. Your brain is much more efficient if well hydrated.

∾

Swimathon

Not quite a swimathon but you're going to make your brain feel like it. Grab your swimsuit and towel and head for the nearest swimming pool. Once you're in, swim lengths in order to really push yourself. If you haven't done any swimming in ages, strive for 10 lengths. If ten lengths is a breeze for you, up the anti. The idea is to move past your usual comfort zone. This will send adrenaline coursing through your body.

∾

Rock and Roll Baby

Put on some rock music and dance like there's no one watching. Mainly because there isn't anyone watching. Unless you're doing this in the park. Then passers bye will be watching you extremely closely and hurrying on by. It's your call. The exercise will get the blood pumping and take more oxygen to your brain. The music will set your brain aflame and have it ready to fight - I mean, write.

∾

A Classic Makeover

After yesterday's frenzied dancing, it's time to take things down a notch or two. Sit down and listen to some classical music. Remember, Bach is extremely good for brain power and motivation. I'm listening to a spot of Bach as I write this. Even if you don't like classical music give this exercise a go. After all, this book is about making changes and allowing your brain to make its own changes.

Red, Red Robin

I know, we've already done the colour red. This isn't about colour but birds. The robin seemed the cutest. Spend a few minutes watching the birds. This is designed for nothing other than to help you relax and take your mind off your writing for a few minutes. Give your brain some time to be creative.

The Grass is Greener

And we've done the colour green. This is about the grass. Find some grass, preferably a large swathe of the natural stuff. Take off your shoes and walk barefoot over it. Feel the coolness or warmth of it depending on where you are. How does it feel to be walking barefoot? What do you notice different about it? How many colours does it contain? I realise it's green but you'll see it's many different colours of green.

21

Dare to be Different

Dare yourself to be different that is. Do something that is right out of your comfort zone. Way beyond anything remotely near your comfort zone. How does it make you feel? Do you have a sense of accomplishment? Were you terrified? Did you feel stupid? Was it exhilarating? Whatever way you feel, channel it into your writing.

War of Worlds

Write a short story in a completely different genre than that in which you usually write. Or write poetry instead of prose. Or introduce some verse into your work in progress. One of the ways in which I do this is to insert humour into my gritty crime books. I've also made a concerted effort to include a bit of romance. Mix it up and change your world.

~

Take a Break

LITERALLY TAKE A BREAK. Either for a couple of days away or even a one-day staycation. If it's a staycation do the things you would usually do on holiday to relax. Buy an ice cream. Go to a café. Read a book. Climb a mountain. Explore the area. The world is your oyster, or at least the small area around you is. The one rule today is:

Have fun.

~

Happy Birthday

You may have to do this one out of synch. If it really is your birthday then I can do magic. If not, either celebrate your real birthday or your writing birthday. Have a glass of something fizzy, please note I am not advocating alcohol although if you want champagne for breakfast have at it and toast the fact that you are awesome. Celebrate you.

~

What Would Burns Do?

Robert Burns, Scotland's very own bard, would write a poem about it. So, today you are going to write a poem. Forty lines on one of the following topics:

1. The writer's life.
2. A whale washed up on the shore.

3. Watching a child sleep.
4. Angels and an argument.

∾

Take the High Road

Climb a hill, or a high building if you live somewhere particularly flat. View your area from a different perspective. How does this change what you see and how you feel? Use these differences to shape your writing. Examining things from a completely different angle can give you a different perspective both physically and in the way you think.

∾

First Catch Your Word

Find a random word in the dictionary and use it to write your next paragraph. You don't have to use the word itself - let its meaning shape your writing.

22

A Word Just for You

ore words? Of course. You are a writer after all. But these words are for you and you alone.

BELIEVE IN YOURSELF.

YOU ARE A HIGHLY TALENTED WRITER.

BELIEVE in yourself and write this affirmation on a sheet of paper.

PIN it above your desk

My Mind's a Blank

Sᴉᴛ down and think of absolutely nothing then come back and read the rest of this. No peeking in advance.

Hᴏᴡ ᴅɪᴅ ᴛʜᴀᴛ ɢᴏ? Impossible. Quite. Your brain would be whirring like a Peregrine Falcon on speed. This is the fastest bird in the world of course. I digress. Use the thoughts that came into your mind whilst you weren't thinking to shape the next few paragraphs of your opus magnum.

~

Jumping Jack

Tɪᴍᴇ ғᴏʀ ᴀ ʙɪᴛ ᴏғ ᴇxᴇʀᴄɪsᴇ. Do some jumping jacks, otherwise known as star jumps. This involves leaping in the air with your hands and legs up like a star. I appreciate everyone might not be able to do this, so do something you can do. If your legs don't work so well just use your arms. Or do some steps using the bottom step in your house. Get that blood pumping. Also, you'll be so busy concentrating on how to do a star jump your brain will forget to be stuck.

~

Be Bold. Be Strong

Bᴇ bold in what you can do. Be bold in writing. Get those fingers on the keyboard and attack it like it's on fire and you are trying to put it out by striking the keys. Write anything even if it's the shopping list. Free write for two minutes and, trust me, your brain will soon move on to the real task in hand. You can always get rid of any extraneous words later.

The Air That I Breathe

STAND OUTSIDE, no matter what the weather, and take 10 deep breaths. How does that feel on your lungs? How does the weather affect your breathing? This has a twofold effect.

1. The fresh air will clear your head.

2. You'll know what your character feels like when breathing deeply in similar circumstances.

YOU CAN TAKE this farther by doing this in several different weather conditions to really get a feel for your character's emotions.

Reach Out

YOU'LL HAVE NOTICED that I haven't said a lot about social media so far and said a lot about putting down your electronics. However, today I am encouraging you to reach out to one other author on social media. Do something nice for them. Examples can be:

Buy one of their books. Tweet about their books. Send an

encouraging word. This is for no other reason than to be nice to someone. You'll feel great.

Stop and Smell the Roses

MORE ROSES, I hear you say. The woman is obsessed with them. It may seem so but it's not the case. Today is all about smell - roses or otherwise. Grab a large sheet of paper and brainstorm all the words you can think of to do with smell or scents. Now find a few more by looking up a dictionary. How has that helped? Good question.

1. You'll have your own mini smell thesaurus.
2. Use one of the words to form the next paragraph of your WIP.

23

In the Stillness

For ten minutes stay completely still. Let the still small voice of your creativity take over. Sometimes we are just too busy and our creativity shuts up and goes back to bed.

We are the Champions

OR YOU ARE. You have been doing these exercises for 150 days now. How do you feel? How has it helped your writing? In what ways is your creativity joining you for a wild ride each day? What have you done differently?

WRITE these below and look back on them when you feel you are struggling.

Texture Matters

USE TOUCH TO explore the world around you. Touch alone. You started life exploring your surroundings by touch, so it's time to do it again. Try different surfaces and textiles. Take them all in properly. What does this tell you about the item that you wouldn't usually think about? Two observations from me:

1. My jumper (or sweater) - the softness of the cashmere, which is almost sensual in its feel. Rather than saying she pulled on a jumper you could say the softness of the wool caressed her tired body and made her feel more alive.

2. The brick wall of my office. It's cold and rough. Use these feelings as someone scrapes himself or herself on a wall. I write crime books so - the freezing, roughness of the wall removed at least two layers of skin, or so he thought.

Taste Success

TREAT yourself to a glass of something fizzy and toast your success. Yes, even before you have reached your goal. Imagine how you will feel when you do this for real.

NOTE, I did not say champagne before you think I'm encouraging you to get tipsy whilst you write.

Give it Up

IF THERE IS anything stopping you writing each day, give it up. One of my biggest failings is that I press the snooze button about a billion times. For you, it might be peering at your mobile phone. Or looking for excuses as to why you can't write.

Let's do it together, starting now.

High Alert

Spend an hour walking around your neighbourhood with all senses on high alert. Pay attention to absolutely everything - sights, sounds, smells. Touch everything you can without the boys in blue coming to fetch you. Taste something from a local bakery or whatever else you fancy. What did you learn? Now your brain is on high alert, use that in your writing.

Mood Altering

No, not drugs. Who do you think I am, for heaven's sake? No laws will be broken in the performing of this exercise. You can use different lights to alter your mood. There you go, that's much more legal. I have a light bulb that changes colour. However, that does involve WiFi and something to control it by voice. You can get bulbs that work with a remote control. Obviously, this will cost money so you may want to think of cheaper ways of changing light colour to alter your mood.

24

Shed a Little Light

Crank up the light in your working space as high as you can. Put on as many lights as you can. If it's a bright sunshiny day, sit outside. You'll find that different amounts of light will alter the way you write. Also, warm light versus cool light can make a difference. This is a simple way to tell your brain that things are different. However, unless you're making millions out of your writing, you may want to think about switching all those lights off at some point.

In the Dark

GOODNESS, I hear you say, this woman is obsessed with lights. Bear with me. Go to the darkest place you can. I mean total darkness. Sit there for ten minutes and take it in. Feel everything around you. What can you make out and how different does it seem? Once you've done that, write a scene where your protagonist is in the dark. How does this change the way they think, feel and act?

If you are claustrophobic or scared of the dark, leave this one alone and repeat one of the other exercises.

Around and Around

The same walk, that is. If your book is set in an area you can easily visit, do a walk around the area. Then do the same route again. And again. What do you notice differently each time? Walk much faster. Walk much more slowly. Do your surroundings seem different? Give your brain the edge by providing several new experiences of the same thing.

Row, Row, Row Your Boat

If it's the right time of year, find somewhere that hires rowing boats and go out on the lake. Not only will you have fun, the exercise will get the oxygen whizzing to your brain and you may get some ideas for your book. Whilst you are rowing pay attention to everything around about you. What do you see differently from this new perspective?

Now, if you will excuse me, I'm off to dump a body. Err, I mean write the next chapter of my crime novel. Honest, your honour. That lake makes a grand body dump.

~

Writing Prompt

YOUR MAIN CHARACTER has just spilt an entire mug of hot coffee down themselves ten minutes before an important meeting.

~

The Colours of the Wind

THIS IS nothing to do with colour - I just like the title - although, you might go blue whilst you are doing it. Go out in the strongest wind you can and walk around. Your main character will usually have to do their job in all weather conditions so this will give you a sense of how this might hamper them.

IF THE WEATHER conditions are a tornado forecast please use common sense. There's no use recreating The Wizard of Oz in real life. Although there is yellow in that.

~

Fruity Frenzy

EAT three different pieces of fruit and enjoy every morsel. Your brain will like the different tastes and the vitamins will also do it good. Even better if you try fruits new to you - Sharon Fruit anyone?

25

The Right Side of the Bed

Or rather the wrong side. You will have to do this tomorrow so read this and skip to the next one. Get out of bed on the opposite side of the bed to the one you usually do. This will tell your brain that things are going to be different today and it will sit up and take notice. It will be begging to know what happens next.

IF THE PERSON you're sharing a bed with clobbers you, your brain will definitely know things are different. Use it to good advantage.

Give Yourself Permission

PERMISSION, to do whatever it takes to change your mindset and get the brain functioning again. No holding back, give it your all, no matter how silly you feel. Your brain is waiting for you to make some changes and to allow it to strut its stuff.

～

A change is as Good as a Rest.

SWITCH IT UP TODAY. Put your current WIP aside and write something totally different. A new challenge for a day will allow your creativity to mix it up and release different ideas. At the same time, it will be percolating new ideas for your original WIP.

ONE CAVEAT. Don't get so carried away with this new project that you forget the original one. The road to Hell is paved with half-finished novels. Or something like that.

～

Look at What You've Done

GO BACK to the notebooks where you jot ideas and possibilities for your writing. You may have written a couple of paragraphs or two to be included in a previous WIP but they didn't make the cut. Can they be used in this one?

～

Dress Differently

REALLY? Yes, really. Change your mindset by changing what you wear. If you always wear head to toe yellow and that's working for you, crack on. In fact, I'm surprised you need this book or are looking at this exercise at all. Unless you're flicking through it in a bookshop but I digress. Change the way you dress. Mix it up and go for something that will shock your brain into changing its ways.

~

Brainstorm

GRAB a huge sheet of paper or tape several A4 sheets together or use a large whiteboard. Brainstorm as many different ideas and words for your book as you possibly can in twenty minutes. Don't think just do. Not sure where to start - write the genre of your book in the middle of the sheet - crime, fantasy, monsters, romance, sci-fi - and use that as a springboard.

~

Free writing

FIND A PEN AND PAPER, no computer for this one. Set a timer for five minutes and write anything you want for five minutes. Even if it's describing the room you're in. No thinking about it, just write. This will get your brain in the mood for writing and free it from junk ready to concentrate on your WIP.

26

Look How Far you've Come

It's time to look at all those achievements again. If you've got writing goals, check where you are with them. What have you achieved in your life, your writing life and your work life? You are a truly amazing human being. Even if all you feel you've achieved is to get up this morning and grab this book, you've achieved so much more than you know. You are taking steps to revolutionise your creative writing.

∾

Let Your Imagination Fly Free

WHAT IS the silliest thing you can think of to write about? I did this exercise myself and came up with an idea for my latest series. I ended up with Cass Claymore, a red-headed, motor-bike riding, ex-ballerina, who inherits a private detective agency and accidentally hires an ex-con dwarf and an octogenarian. The first book, *Antiques and Alibis* was published a year ago and fans love it. You never know where the silliest ideas will take you.

∼

Ready, Steady, Write

GRAB your computer or notebook and open it to your WIP. Set a timer for five minutes and write for five minutes. No editing. No stopping. Just writing.

WALK AROUND THE ROOM.

REPEAT THE ABOVE FIVE TIMES.

∼

A Different Perspective

LOOK at your city from different perspectives. Go down into a vault or basement if you can. Look at it from buildings of different heights. Go on to the roof of buildings. What different ideas does this give you? What if your characters were in the vault? How easy is it to escape? A rooftop chase? Is this possible? See how you can work it into your WIP.

∼

Read a Newspaper

YOU CAN GET all sorts of ideas for stories from reading the local paper. If it's a newly minted crime you might not want to use it as a basis of a story as that is taking advantage of others misfortune. However, there are other things. For example, I read the story of Christian McLaggan and Scotland's Lost Broch. This became the basis for my YA book, *The Dagger's Curse*. You never know where inspiration might strike next.

~

We All Stand Together

MEET up with some writer friends. Have coffee and enjoy spending time together. If you want to discuss your work, go for it. If not, just enjoy. Relaxing will give your brain space to catch up.

~

Look to the City

TAKE A TRIP INTO THE CITY. Look at all the different buildings and how they fit together. Have you ever wondered why they've grown like this? Why they have been built the way they have. Write down all the different types of buildings, what they are made from, colours, door types. Use this to add richness to your writing.

YOU CAN TAKE this further by researching the history of some of the buildings and use some of this in your WIP.

27

David Bailey - You What?

Yes, we've already done our David Bailey exercise. However, today you are going to take photographs inside your home. Get in close and take photos of different objects. Put the photos up on a big screen. What is different about them? Can you see textures more clearly? Colours? Light, dark, shade? How can this help you develop richer writing without overwhelming the reader with detail?

USE two of the photos as a fifty-word piece of flash fiction.

The Scent of Success

APPARENTLY SMELLING ORANGE, vanilla and cinnamon can enhance creativity. Mints can also give the brain a pep talk and get it to pay much closer attention. So, time to crack out the scented candles and suck on some mints.

IF YOU'LL EXCUSE ME, I'm off to go shopping.

~

The Past is the Past

OR IS IT? Surprisingly, or maybe not so surprisingly, history can provide much inspiration for contemporary fiction. Or, inspiration for non-fiction. Choose a historical non-fiction book from your shelf, the bookshop or the library. Take notes and jot down ideas. Use one of them in your WIP. You'll learn a lot in the process.

~

Stand up for Yourself

THIS IS a bit of a sneaky title as it doesn't involve fighting. Yes, I know you were up for a scrap but I don't advocate violence. Today's writing will involve alternating between standing and sitting to write. This will give your brain different perspectives and therefore allow it to think differently. It is also healthier for you.

IF YOU STRUGGLE TO STAND, I'm not excluding you. Either visualise yourself standing to write – the brain is a powerful thing – or do a different exercise.

~

Magazines Matter

YOU'D BE AMAZED at the things you can find in magazines that will spark your imagination. Trust me, there are all sorts in there. I got an idea for one that I am using in my current WIP which is a humorous crime book. Today's motivation will be found by buying three magazines and reading them. Motivating yourself can take many different forms and be lots of fun.

∽

Stop Right Now

IT'S time for a day off. Do absolutely no writing whatsoever today. Just rest and enjoy. You'll feel mentally and physically better for it.

∽

Early to Rise

YESTERDAY YOU HAD a day off and today you are going to get up as early as you can and write before you do anything else. Oh, go on then, you can make coffee first. Your brain will be galvanised into action with all this chopping and changing. It won't have time to think about the fact it's meant to be stuck, it will be too busy trying to catch up with what you are doing. Plus, the peace will help you think better.

28

Move Yourself

Grab a digital voice recorder or mobile, anything with a voice recorder will do. Spend an hour walking around and dictating. This can be your house if you feel too much of a prat to do it outside. We are oral storytellers after all. That's how storytelling started, passing down through the generations. Speaking out loud can help you to draw your thoughts together. You can then type this into your WIP or transfer it using text to print software. You can even dictate it straight into a word processor, for example, Microsoft Word for mobile.

Listen to the Children

YEP, time to borrow some children again. Listen to the way they talk and the way they boil everything down to basics. Listen to how they talk as they play, how they communicate with each other and how they communicate with you. Listen to their speech patterns and the cadence of their voices. How does it make you feel? Are the shrieks or shrill tones giving you a migraine? Does their laughter fill you with joy?

Use this new found knowledge to strengthen your writing giving it more depth and colour.

Sight and Sound

Firstly, close your eyes and only take in the world using sound. You may not hear anything at first but keep those eyes closed until you pick up the background noises you would ordinarily tune out.

Once you have done that, block your ears off with earplugs. Take in the world using only your eyes.

How different does this feel?

True to Type

You're probably beginning to realise that none of the chapter titles are what they seem at first. Good, as that's the idea. To get your brain wondering what's coming next.

.   .   .

TRACK down a good old-fashioned typewriter and use that to type your work today. No, I've no idea how you're going to do that but won't it be fun trying.

~

Let it Go

I BET you've got that song pounding around in your head now. I certainly have. Still, plough through. This exercise is designed to make you think hard about whether you're stuck because this manuscript is not going to go anywhere. It's a good question to ask yourself – is it time to let it go and move on with another project.

WAIT A MINUTE; aren't you meant to be motivating me, not encouraging me to quit? Absolutely, but asking yourself this question will force your brain to think in a different way. You never know, the perfect solution might come along whilst your concentration is elsewhere.

~

A Toast to Yourself

POUR YOURSELF A DRINK, preferably at a time when it's more acceptable to be swigging alcohol. Use your best crystal glasses and celebrate how far you've come as a writer. The fact you are sitting at a keyboard, or have bought a nice notebook, means you are further ahead than most people who think about writing a novel. You are awesome. You are an awesome writer. I believe in you. Believe in yourself. Cheers.

The Wisdom of Trees

You've moved off into the half-baked realm, I hear you say. Batty as they come. You would think so but bear with me, I've not let you down yet.

First find your tree – a really old and tall one. Preferably with spreading branches and lots of leaves. Lie down under it and contemplate life. Let your thoughts drift and take in the beauty and grandeur and splendour of what is above you. Take in the light pattern and let it relax you and settle your thoughts. You'll find the wisdom of the world will come to you.

29

The Water Rushes By

Find some fast flowing water. I'm talking really fast flowing here. Not possible - do your best. If you live near Niagara Falls then you're cooking on gas. Otherwise find the fastest river you can. Listen to the sound of the rushing water and think about what it would feel like to be swept away. Write down all your feelings, especially visceral fear, and use this when writing to develop characters more fully.

Bathing Beauty

CRACK out your swimsuit or swimming trunks, it's time to go swimming. Use a local pool, or a stream or the sea, wherever you feel most comfortable and spend 30 minutes swimming. It will clear your head, give you thinking time and you'll also be fitter than you were. You win every which way.

~

What can you Smell?

THERE ARE two ways of doing this.

1. Ask someone in the house to blindfold you and then put various scents under your nose. What can you smell? How easy is it to identify things by smell alone?

2. Go to a park, the countryside or the beach. Close your eyes and spend time using smell alone. What different scents are coming through?

WRITING IS RICHER when all the senses are used. However, we often forget smell when writing.

~

Air Your Grievances

YOU MIGHT WANT to do this one when you are home alone with the windows shut. I'm not telling you to pick a fight with anyone. Use the largest room in your house. Pace around it and shout as loud as you can about how difficult it is being stuck. How you hate writing and why life is unfair. Now spend five minutes shouting why it's so wonderful. You don't want to finish on a down note. I bet you feel much better now.

~

Bounce

TIME TO GO BACK to your childhood and bounce on a trampoline. You can't seem to move for trampolines in people's gardens these days, so you should have no trouble borrowing one. Simply enjoy the feeling of being young again. Let me tell you, your brain will be doing somersaults, even if you're not. It will be galvanised and ready for action when you sit down at your computer.

BEFORE ANYONE BREAKS a leg during this exercise, you can sit on the trampoline or your bed and bounce that way. Trips to A&E with broken bones do tend to eat into one's writing time.

Snowball Fight

ONE FOR THE winter - literally go and have a snowball fight with your friends. Enjoy the exhilaration of running around in the snow and dodging snowballs. Your brain will be taking in the cold and the way you are feeling. At the same time, all that oxygen whizzing around will fire up the old grey cells.

WHEN YOU RETURN to the computer, hot drink in hand, you'll be buzzing and ready to write up a storm.

In the Street Where I live

SPEND fifteen minutes walking up and down your street, really taking in all the details. You might think you live in a street with identical houses but I can absolutely guarantee you don't. Something will be different in every single house. You'll find you are so familiar with your street you take nothing in. It's time to change that and train your brain to start noticing.

30

Ballet Moves

Y ou can go the whole hog on this one, or merely a few steps. Did you know, there are ballet classes for every age group, up to senior citizens. If you feel like making a big change then why not join one. No? Okay, just a few steps then. Do a search on YouTube for basic ballet steps and then do at least five. What does this do to motivate me? Good question. Remember what I said at the beginning of the book. Make a change for a change.

One Finger in Front of the Other

THIS IS brilliant for kick-starting the imagination. Use finger puppets, or larger puppets and make up a children's story using them. That seems like a lot of expense to me, I hear you say. I borrowed some from my local library. Trust me, libraries can help you out with anything. They truly are magical places.

Writing Prompt

THIS IS A DO it yourself writing prompt. Draw a doodle in the space below and write a short story about it, or include it in your current novel.

Look at it from the Other Side

THIS IS easy where I live, as my city is on one side of a large river. I can go over the bridge and look at the city from the other side. You get a totally different viewpoint doing this. Use your imagination to think of a way to change perspective on your city and see it with new eyes. What do you see that hasn't entered your consciousness before?

Put it to One Side

FOR ONE DAY ONLY, put your WIP aside and work on something else. I mean something completely different - a poem, a piece of flash fiction, change of genre, historical, non-fiction - anything that's different.

Your Brain Will Believe

ANYTHING YOU TELL it to believe. Bounce up in the morning and before you have time to think, tell yourself this is going to be an awesome writing day. Tell your brain you are going to write 1,000 words before breakfast and it will be on the starting block waiting for the starting pistol to fire.

Ice Cream

BUY an ice cream and spend fifteen minutes sitting down enjoying it. Savour every minute, then work out how you can have your characters eating ice cream in your current work. I managed it in a crime book, so I'm sure you can do it in yours. Unless your book is about travelling across the arctic tundra, in which case you need to work that one out yourself.

31

Five-Minute Sprints

Set a timer for five minutes and do a five-minute writing sprint. At the end of five minutes, take deep breaths and start again. No editing. Just writing. At the end of an hour look at how many words you have written. You will be amazed. Your brain will be too busy writing to think about being stuck.

Think About it

SPEND ten minutes writing down a plan of what you are going to write for the day. Pin the plan up somewhere you can see it.

ONCE YOU HAVE DONE THAT, start writing.

Or Don't

I SAID you would be mixing things up so your brain is constantly on high alert and excited. Today, you will do the complete opposite to yesterday's exercise. Write without planning anything. Carry on from where you left off yesterday. Your brain will continue the process as it will have been quietly working out a plan whilst you weren't looking. Brains are sneaky things.

~

A Great Height

No, we haven't done this before. Grab a step and do ordinary tasks as though you are taller. I am quite short and often have to grab a step to reach things higher up. Sometimes I fill the teabag canister whilst I am still on the step. It's amazing how different it feels doing it as a person who is apparently taller. This is a good one for getting to know how characters of different heights might do things.

~

A New Book

NOT WRITE A NEW BOOK, buy a new book. Reward yourself by reading a couple of chapters when you have written a certain number of words for the day. Then repeat.

YOU'LL BE AMAZED at how well you write when there's a reward at the end of it.

A Different Blend

No sneaking in something different here, this really is a different blend. Of tea or coffee that is. Buy a different blend than you normally use. I'm not talking about make - blend. How about trying some Assam or Orange Pekoe tea or a blend of coffee from a different country. That will definitely shock your brain into realising today is different.

Now if you'll excuse me, I'm off to open my new packet of Cuban coffee and brew a nice pot.

Strip it Down

No, not you! You'll freeze to death doing that. Strip your book down to the basics. Write an elevator pitch. What do you mean, that's hard? Of course it is. That's the whole idea. When you've finished, sitting down to write your novel will be a breeze.

32

Writing Prompt

An off duty firefighter is walking along the street with his ten-year-old daughter. He sees a burning building with a toddler at the window. He doesn't have a phone with him.

Do be Daft

THE USUAL MANTRA is don't be daft. Mix it up and be as daft as you like. Do something extremely silly and let your hair down. Let go of your inhibitions and let that wild side take over.

Write it Down

IF THERE IS something bothering you that is stopping you from writing, write it down. Every last detail. Now put it to one side for later. This will free your mind so your thoughts can move on to what is important right now, which is carrying on with your writing.

~

Write it Down Differently

Is yesterday's problem still bothering you? Write it down differently. Your subconscious will chew it over whilst you get on with the important business of carrying on with the real writing.

~

Dance Like no one is Watching

YES, more dancing. Also, there isn't anyone watching. Dancing is a fantastic way to fire up your creativity because you are using a different part of your creative brain. It's also a great deal of fun and good exercise so you gain all round.

~

Stretch Yourself

STRETCH yourself physically by completing five stretching exercises each morning. Writing is a sedentary occupation and it's easy to slip into a lifestyle where exercise gets shoved out.

STRETCH yourself mentally by doing a mental writing exercise before you start for the day. Five minute free writing is a good way to start.

~

It's all a Jumble

SOMETIMES THE REASON you struggle to write is because your thoughts are all jumbled up. They are whirling around in your head like bingo balls. It's time to straighten them out and get them in some order. Use a large whiteboard or flipchart paper. Spend twenty minutes writing down every possible idea that presents itself. Use different coloured pens.

NOW THAT THEY are out there, spend ten minutes putting them into some semblance of order.

33

Pick up the Pen. Put Down the Pen

S pend ten minutes writing by hand. Put down the pen. Spend ten minutes writing using the computer. Pick up the pen and spend ten minutes handwriting.

YOU GET THE PICTURE.

Let the Breeze in About You

THAT'S what my mother used to say when I was young. The idea was, getting out in the fresh air was healthy. I agree, it certainly is healthy, both mentally and physically. Take a walk and feel the breeze and the air on your skin. Take deep breaths, unless you're walking up a street jam-packed with cars. Then you might want to rethink the deep breathing part.

Let the breeze and the fresh air blow away the cobwebs and

allow your mind to be filled with lovely thoughts of your current project.

Hair Today

IT'S time to do something hair raising. Something you wouldn't normally do. If this is something that would take planning then, what are you waiting for, start your plan. If it is easily done, what are you waiting for?

You Can't be Serious

MAKE your character do something completely stupid. Something they would never ordinarily do. For example, make your detective hide evidence or walk over the crime scene. See where that story twist can take you.

Think for a Minute

SIT at the keyboard hands poised, or with a notebook in front of you and your pen at the ready. Set a timer for one minute and think about what you are going to write. When the timer bell goes start writing without pausing. Your brain will see it as a natural progression and won't miss a heartbeat. This is also a superb way to get your word count up.

Listen to Your Heart

VERY OFTEN YOU may be stuck because you are overthinking things. We humans have a tendency to do this. Listen to what your heart is telling you to write. If it means your two main characters splitting up, do it. See where the story, and your heart, takes you.

Get up and Get Going

IF YOU ARE anything like me you will press the snooze umpteen times in the morning. You'll then prevaricate for some time before you get going. It's time to make changes. When the alarm goes off get straight out of bed. After you've brushed your teeth and made coffee, stagger to yourwork space and start writing. No checking social media or looking at emails. Immediately start writing.

IF YOU ALREADY DO THIS, you're a hero and I want to be you.

34

You What?

Listen to what your characters are telling you to do. If a new character strolls in, give them free rein and see how they develop. One of the main characters in my *Cass Claymore Investigates* series came about that way. It turns out the women love Quill, both in the book and in the real world. Go figure.

∼

Taste and See That it is Good

Eat something you've never eaten in your life before. I try to do this when I go to new countries which has led me to eating some extremely exotic dishes. So, think of something you haven't eaten and give it a go today.

I'm off to try some sushi, which I've resisted until now.

~

Make a Difference

Do something to help someone else today. Make a difference in their life.

WHAT'S that got to do with writing, I hear you ask? Absolutely nothing but you will have made another person's life just that little bit better. Life isn't all about writing.

~

Challenge Yourself

SET a challenge to write a certain amount of words today. Even if you have a really busy day, make it an outrageous amount. Once completed, plan out how you are going to do it. Plan the time in your diary. Use every spare minute to write, wherever you may be or whatever you are doing.

~

Writing Prompt

IT WAS Christmas day at precisely 3 pm when I realised that...

~

Where will it End

WRITE the ending of your book. It may change but at least your brain will know the end is in sight. It may also give you an idea of where the saggy middle might be going. If you're feeling stuck, I can almost certainly guarantee it's that pesky saggy middle causing problems.

The Ayes Have It

SPEND the day saying yes and see where it takes you. Yes, to new ideas. Yes to taking the kids to the zoo. Yes to coffee with a friend. Yes to someone taking the kids off your hands for a couple of hours. Yes to a new writing project. The sky's your limit. Or should I say the ayes your limit?

35

An Emotional Connection

Spend thirty minutes thinking about your main character's emotions and motivations. Jot down notes, even if it's just words, colours, their thoughts, no matter how inconsequential you feel it might be. In the middle of this there will be nuggets you can use right at the precise moment they are needed.

From the Sublime to the Ridiculous

WRITE a scene which has your character doing something quite mundane. Immediately follow this up with them doing something completely ridiculous, or have something strange happen. The abrupt change of direction will get your readers sitting up and wondering what's going on, as will your brain.

Freewriting Freedom

FREEWRITING IS a great way to get your brain not only moving but firing on all four cylinders. So, another ten minutes of free writing and then straight on to your WIP.

Flavours of Mexico

OR FLAVOURS of anywhere you fancy. Write something exotic into your current scene. How does this change things, does it inspire you to go in a different direction? Does it make your brain say that's not the way it's meant to happen and change everything again? You'll either write a cracking scene or untangle yourself and head in the right direction again with an equally cracking scene. What have you got to lose?

Missed Connection

YOU MAY BE STUCK because you've missed a connection somewhere. Using a large sheet of paper, backtrack on what you've written and draw out a map of the connections you've made. What's the missing link?

Take Words Out

YES, you heard me right. Cut the last paragraph and paste it onto another sheet of paper.

. . .

NOW REWRITE THE SCENE AGAIN. Is this better or worse? Has it helped you solidify your thoughts? Are you going in a different direction?

NOW CARRY on with the story. If you prefer the original paragraph, you can always copy and paste it back again.

Off the Grid

OFF THE ELECTRICITY grid that is. No, I'm not asking you to move to the mountains and become a prepper. That's some imagination you've got. You do, however, have to take yourself to the middle of nowhere. Take a pen and notebook and move somewhere you can't get a signal on your phone. Spend the day writing in a totally different environment in order to focus the mind.

I'M off to find a shepherd's hut - an easy task in Bonnie Scotland.

36

_____

Brain Switch

You need to move from the left (logical) side of your brain and switch to the right (creative) side of your brain. Did you know Sodoku uses both sides of your brain? Find one in a daily newspaper, or download one from the Internet and spend time completing it.

Blowing Hot and Cold

LITERALLY BLOWING HOT AND COLD. Use a fan heater to blow hot air at you and write. Now turn it to cold and carry on writing. Now hot. Now cold. Once you've done three cycles of this stop and have a break. Did you write differently during hot spells or cold spells? Did either interfere with your ability to write? One thing it will do is keep your brain on high alert banishing any signs of sleepiness.

Pump up the Volume

PLAY some music and pump up the volume. This will keep you awake, especially if it's around 140 beats per minute. Obviously, you don't want to do this while you're writing but do it for 10 minutes beforehand. Your pulse will be up and your brain active - the perfect conditions for writing up a storm.

Writing Prompt

I STUMBLED to my computer and was confronted by a note. My heart thumped more loudly as I read the words.

Time for a Break

ALL WORK MAKES JACK, or Jill, a dull boy, or girl. Off you go and enjoy yourself.

Endless Fun

WRITING SHOULD BE fun and yet, you may be feeling all the joy has gone out of it. Time to have a bit of fun. Use the space at the bottom to brainstorm fun things your characters could do. Yes, even the serial killer. No one is completely bad.

Roses Grow on You

WE'RE BACK TO ROSES. Actually, we're not. Unless you want to, that is. Do some gardening. Whilst you are digging about in the soil, I can guarantee your thoughts will be on your WIP. You may be dreaming of how you can murder someone. Have at it. Unless you're writing a children's picture book, in which case you might want to stop yourself going down that route.

37

Pay Attention Now

Spend time paying attention to everything around you - sights, sounds, smell, touch, taste - rather than wandering through the day like a zombie. Humans do tend to get into a rut and starting today you are going to step out of that rut and move in a different direction.

Motivation Matters

THINK about the title of this book. It's a play on words. It can mean Motivation is important or it can mean these are matters pertaining to motivation. Even the title of the book is a motivational tool. How can you use this knowledge in your own writing?

History is a Mystery

FIND a historical fact and use it as the basis of a piece of flash fiction or a short story in the genre of mystery. Or include it as a mystery in your novel.

∾

A Level Playing Field

IN FACT, find any playing field level or otherwise. Grab a group of friends and play a game outside. I don't know about where you live but here in Scotland, we have free tennis courts, football pitches, bowling greens, golf courses etc. Get out and have fun. Now, how would it change the dynamics in your novel if your characters did a similar thing? At least you'll have some fodder to write a stupendous scene.

∾

Writing Prompt

AT THE MOMENT THEY KISSED...

∾

Baby, Baby

WRITE a scene using a baby as the main character. You may not want to use it now but keep it safe in a file. You never know when it might come in useful.

. . .

IF IT HAS SPARKED an idea for you to continue with your current WIP - happy days.

Look Hear

THE GRAMMAR NAZI within is probably screaming right now. However, shoot it. Or at least tell it to shut up. You are going to both look and listen today. When you are speaking to someone, listen to them properly and watch their facial expressions carefully. Not only will you respond more closely but you will be able to make your writing richer.

38

Ramp it Up

That is, ramp up the tension in your novel. Already writing a tense scene? Take it up a notch or two. Is your heart beating faster and can you feel the tension in your stomach? If the answer is yes, you've cracked it. Your readers will feel exactly the same way. Plus lashings of adrenaline will make your writing flow faster.

Shout it Out

CLOSE ALL THE windows and doors. Walk around the house and shout out ideas for the story. Use a digital voice recorder to record these ideas. Use one of them to move the next part of your story forward. Come on now, don't be shy.

A Rare Find

TAKE a walk along the beach and look for objects or unusual pieces of driftwood. Sit down on the sand and study them. How could they be used in your manuscript?

NOWHERE NEAR A BEACH. Do a similar exercise using a forest. You could use a beech instead of a beach. Pun intended.

Pink and Even More Pink

THIS IS ABOUT THE COLOUR, not the singer. Although you can make it about both if you want. Today, look around you for the colour pink. Trust me, it will be in more places than you can ever possibly imagine. From sunrise to sunset, you'll be tripping over it everywhere. It's time to paint the town pink.

Sunnier Side of the Street

LOOK for sunlight and shadow as you walk around. How does different light change the look, feel and texture of buildings? Or a street, park, car or any object you see? How can you use this to good effect in your WIP? Could it be a clue in a crime novel? Hide, or light up, lovers in a romance? Give an angel a halo or change a dragon from sinister to magnificent in one swift flick of a sunbeam? Use light more effectively to ensure your writing is four-dimensional.

Name It

TIME TO EXPLORE NAMES AGAIN. Not character names this time but naming the things blocking you. In a long list, down the left-hand side of the page, write down anything stopping you from writing. Once you're finished, on the right-hand side, write down all the things you can do to change the negatives. Implement them one at a time. It may start out as an elephant but soon it will be the size of a tadpole.

Sing it Out

SING the next two paragraphs of your work, to the tune of a favourite song. The music and words together will help you to think more clearly and you will be able to move forward with some great ideas.

39

Catch the Wave

Firstly, catch the wave by spending some time jumping over waves. Of course, this is if you have access to a beach or wave pool. If not, use a jump rope and do some skipping.

ONCE YOU HAVE HAD a lot of fun and some exercise, catch the wave of creativity released by all those lovely endorphins.

Let's Get Together

GET TOGETHER with some friends and have a writers' retreat. Even if this is just for a day, go away somewhere and spend time together writing. You will find you spur each other on and can hold each other accountable.

Boogie Wonderland

FIND the song *Boogie Wonderland* by Earth Wind and Fire. Play it loud and sing and dance along. Who can fail to get all those happy endorphins flowing when this is playing? I found it on YouTube, Apple Music and Amazon Music so it's not difficult to track it down.

Writing Prompt

IT WAS AXEL'S BIRTHDAY. I do remember that clearly.

SUBSTITUTE the name Axel for a character in your book.

A Gathering of Clouds

I SPEND a lot of time looking at clouds. Mainly because I am always worried they'll appear the minute I hang washing out. In your case, lay a blanket on the ground, lie on it and spend some time watching the clouds. Look for pictures in them. What can you see? What stories can you make up about them?

WHAT WAS that you were saying about your imagination having dried up?

Choose a Number

CHOOSE the number of words you will write today. To get you going here are some to choose from. Circle the one you want to reach.

145
380
500
750
1000
3000
10000

Look for the Good

LOOK for people doing good deeds today - there will be a lot more than you think. It will restore your faith in humankind and will give you ideas for your novel. Use these to shape your character. Even if you are writing the worst villain ever imagined, he can still rescue an old lady's cat or do his old ma's shopping.

40

Look to the Animals

Spend the day watching animals. Any animals. There are loads out there. How many different animals do you see as you go about your daily life? Today, doing nothing out of the ordinary I've seen a heron, ducks, wood pigeon, crows, a badger, a fox, cows, calves, horses, llamas and a field mouse. The field mouse was obviously playing chicken as it ran out in front of my car. I slowed down and let it carry on its merry little way. How could an exercise such as this, revolutionise your writing?

Bare it All

I'M NOT ADVOCATING your birthday suit, but do wear a lot less than you would usually. Now write. See how changing just one habit can give the old brain an electric shock and allow it to change your thought patterns. This will translate into your writing.

Any Questions

Ask yourself five questions about possible directions for your WIP. Write them down and then answer them. Use one of the answers to form the next part of your work. Keep the others for an emergency when you can whip them out and use one of them to resuscitate that saggy middle.

Mellow Yellow

It's yellow's turn to be scrutinised. You know the drill. Ready, steady, find as many instances of the colour yellow as you can in one day. This is an easy one as I can see at least six without moving from my office chair. There are four on my computer menu bar before I even start.

Writing Prompt

Use these four words as a short story, poem, flash fiction or for the next part of your WIP.

Flash
Genius
Form
Post-Its

∼

I Feel the Need

You got it - the need for speed.
Run up and down on the spot for five minutes. Go as fast as you can.
Type as fast as you can for fifteen minutes. No stopping. No editing. Just typing.
What's your word count? I can guarantee you'll be pleasantly surprised.

∼

Before you go any Further

Read your last two paragraphs. Take notes on ways you think the story could move from there. Use one of them and start writing.

41

Catalyst

Please do not muck about with chemicals to cause a catalytic reaction. Instead, eat a piece of chocolate, which will release happy chemicals into your bloodstream. Not only will you enjoy it but it will also bring new vigour to your attitude and your work. Chocolate always makes everything feel better.

Hot, Hot, Hot

CRANK UP the heat and pretend you are in the tropics. Unless you are in the tropics of course, in which case go outside. Write a scene where your character is enjoying the heat or is hot and uncomfortable. Use it as a plot twist in your book whilst ensuring the descriptions of how he or she feels is spot on. Two for the price of one.

Work Hard. Play Harder

THINK of something you really enjoy doing and which is a rare treat. Write it down as a promise to yourself - when you get three-quarters of the way through the manuscript the treat will be ripe for the taking. This should get you rattling through the middle, saggy or otherwise. Take time out and honour your promise. Enjoy every minute.

Turn the Page

TURN the page of a good book, one not in your usual genre and spend the day reading. Notice which conventions are different and which are the same. Widening your reading choices helps make you a better writer.

Nice Writing

TAKE a look back over what you have written. Notice the areas you have done particularly well and compliment yourself. I am sure you have got the beating yourself up area off to a fine art. However, how many times do you compliment yourself? It's time to tell your brain it's doing an awesome job.

Out With the Old

NOT COMPLETELY OUT with the old as you might throw out some nuggets of gold. However, crack open a brand new notebook and grab a new pen. The very fact everything is new will allow your brain to draw a line under the old ways of thinking - including the fact it was in the doldrums. A new notebook always inspires creativity.

～

K.I.S.S

WHEN I WAS in the army we were taught the K.I.S.S. principle - keep it simple stupid. One of the big reasons for failure is over-complicating things. Keep your words and your plan simple and you'll find your writing starts to flow again. There is time to make it more complex when you edit.

42

Writing Prompt

I t's always the smallest detail that finds you...

It's a Large Stretch

STRETCH HAS many connotations -

1. A piece of land.
2. A spell in prison.
3. Pulling an item to make it longer.
4. Seeing something way out in front of you
5. Reaching over for something.

How can analysing words like this help develop your writing?

Stamp Stamp

You can stamp around the house if you want to, it will make you feel much better. However, this exercise is aimed at creative stamping. Borrow some rubber stamps and spend an hour enjoying another creative activity. The more use you make of the creative side of your brain, the more alert it will be.

REMEMBER MY USUAL MANTRA, your local library will probably have some you can use. If not - call a friend.

I want to Break Free

BREAK FREE from the shackles of your desk. Think of the most unusual place you could do some writing, go there and write. I've written at the Captain's table on a historic ship amongst many other places. One caveat; do ask permission as you might get more publicity than you ever wanted when you are arrested. This is not the rock and roll scene.

Mind out Now

IT's time for a spot of visualisation. Think of a goal you would like to reach with your writing. It may be writing a thousand words, writing The End on your current WIP or selling a million copies. It doesn't matter, as the goal is personal. Picture yourself achieving this goal. What does it feel like? What are the sights, smells, sounds? Can you hear the crowds roar? Can you see yourself celebrating? Can you smell the sweet scent of champagne? Feel the bubbles tickle your nose?

OVER TO YOU.

Musical Chairs

A SIMPLE ONE TODAY. Change the chair you usually sit on to write. If it's an office chair - use a hardback. If it's a hardback - sit on the sofa. Heck, sit on a garden chair or a deck chair. Just move chairs. Make a change for a change.

In a Nutshell

WRITE DOWN, in a nutshell, what is bothering you. Don't spend a lot of time doing this. Strip it down to as few words as possible. Now look at it and tell yourself how inconsequential it really is in the grand scheme of things. I am not trivialising your feelings here and if your issue is huge, then you need to deal with it differently but often you'll find it's merely the brain playing tricks.

43

Trip the Light Fantastic

Write in different levels of light. Writing this book I have used my bright office light, written outside in glorious sunshine in the Caribbean, switched the light off in my office, written on a plane with no light at all except the backlight of my computer. The rest of the cabin was asleep. Different lights can give you a different perspective.

Value added

THERE'S ALWAYS VALUE ADDED, especially in this book, as I often give you more than one outcome from the exercise. Think of something that could happen to your character and the way in which it could affect him or her. Maybe it affects them in more than one way. Or maybe they did the right thing but it led to a bad outcome. Think of ways in which you can write a sentence which lends itself to different interpretations.

Mars Attack

IT DOESN'T HAVE to be Mars - any chocolate will do. Not too much of course. I don't want the blame for your weight gain.

Now, write 100 words on mounting an attack on Mars. Watch those grey cells sizzle.

Message in a Bottle

WRITE a message to yourself about how you are feeling right now. Put it in a bottle and metaphorically chuck it in the sea - the oceans have enough rubbish in them without me advocating you add to it. Put the bottle away and carry on writing. Take it out in one month and read it. How has your perspective changed during the month?

What's in a Word

YEP, we've done this one before but it is worth repeating. Lose yourself in the beauty and wonder of words. Take the original piece of flipchart paper out and grab a thesaurus. Add to the list you started in exercise twelve. Haven't you come a long way since then.

Autumn Leaves

THIS REALLY IS one for autumn. Find a pile of autumn leaves and jump around in them like you did when you were a kid. Look at the colours on the trees and on the leaves on the ground. Take notes for use when writing a scene set in autumn. Another value added for you.

Pat-a-Cake

IT's time to bake a cake. Even if you are short of time, buy a cake making kit and anything else you need to add. Mix it up, pop it in the oven, set a timer and write whilst you are waiting for it to cook. Write furiously whilst the cake is baking. Take it out of the oven. Write up a storm. Cut a slice of cake, make a cup of coffee and have a well-earned break.

THAT's my recipe for a great writing day.

44

Stretching the Truth

No, it's not time to lie but you may want your main character to tell a lie. Yes, I know they're the most upright citizen on the planet but this will make the fact even more shocking. It will also shape the way they think and do things for the remainder of the book.

Just five minutes More

WHEN YOU GET to the end of your writing day, write for just five minutes more. See how many more words you can get in during those five minutes.

You'll be amazed by how fast and furiously your fingers fly over the keyboard.

Early Morning

GET up with the birds and listen to them welcome the day. As I write this I can hear birds tweeting outside. It's a marvellous sound and I'm tapping away before anyone else is awake. It's peaceful and there's no one to disturb me. Plan to get up early tomorrow and see how much you can write before the day really gets going.

~

A New Day is Dawning

NO MATTER how stuck you may feel, get up telling yourself it's a brand new day. One where your brain is alert and eager to start writing. Your brain will believe whatever you tell it to believe. Clatter straight to your writing desk and get started. No prevarication allowed. Trust me your brain will join you a whooping and a hollering and ready to crack on.

~

Rest and be Thankful

TODAY IS A REST DAY. Take time out and enjoy being you.

~

Childhood Memories

THINK OF A FAVOURITE CHILDHOOD MEMORY. How does it make you feel? Why is it a favourite? What were you doing? Imagine you are there again.

. . .

TAKE that happy feeling and translate it into your writing. You can't fail to write right when you are feeling all right.

I Have a Dream

EVERY TIME you have a dream write it down the minute you wake up. Every detail you can remember. My first book started with a dream. No, not the first chapter. I know that's an unwritten rule, no opening with dreams. However, the idea came from a dream and ended up as a three-hundred-page novel. That's some dream.

45

It's all About You

Today is all about you. Do something to pamper yourself and celebrate you. After all, there is no other you in the world. You are unique and uniquely special.

∾

Imagination Station

GRAB A NOTEBOOK AND PEN, put some background music on and let your imagination fly free. Write down every single little detail that comes into your mind. Build an ideas bank that you can use at times where you don't know where to go next. I use Evernote on my phone, computer and iPad to write notes like this. Then it's only a matter of looking it up on whatever device I am using.

∾

Poets Corner

SPEND TODAY PENNING A POEM. I'm no poet either but the very act of doing this will use a different creative part of your brain. The more of the brain you use regularly, the more alert it will become and the more of it you will use.

Stationery

BUY some stationery to help you move forward. It's amazing what a lovely notebook and a brand new pen can do to help you write again. The minute you've bought it, go into a coffee shop, find a comfortable chair and start writing. You might want to buy a coffee or something first, otherwise, the proprietors might get a little antsy.

STATIONERY CAN HELP you stop being stationary.

Writing Prompt

USING pink paper was not my idea of the best way to pen my opus magnum. Blood red was more my style. Yet I was reduced to pink.

Bear Necessities

READ a Winnie-the-Pooh book and examine how much

wisdom is packed into a simple story. Using words to good effect, A.A. Milne wrote stories that appealed to both children and adults. Your local library calls again.

Ice Cold In

EAT an ice-lolly before you start writing today. Not the type that is a glorified ice cream, but a real fruit lolly. Feel the cold ice trickle down your throat and savour the flavours. Your brain will be on high alert, especially if you're eating this ice-lolly at the crack of dawn. And, in a two for one, you'll have enjoyed a nice ice-lolly.

46

From the High, High, Highlands

Visit one of the highest points in your area. I'm told even The Netherlands has a hill. You'll have a pleasant day out, get to know more of the surrounding area, examine the geography and terrain and do a spot of writing elsewhere. It's a grand day out all around.

Way Down Low

SIT on the floor and write today. What, I hear you say? I encourage you to go with the flow and do daft things. You've been doing them for the last three-hundred-and-ten days so why should today be any different. Mix it up and your brain will join in.

Way up High

YOU'VE GOT IT. Write way up high today. Sit on the top step in the house, or even the top of a stepladder. A change is as good as a kick up the writing bahookie.

Writing Prompt

RAINDROPS KEEP FALLING ON ...

Travel the World

COME BACK. Stop packing that backpack. It's metaphorical travel. Now you've got over your disappointment, grab a map and push a pin in a random spot on a map of the world.

WHEREVER IT IS, take your character there. Yes, I really do mean it. Off you go.

Reach for the Stars

FOOLED YOU. We're not going back to the white twinklies in the sky but pop stars. Write a scene where a famous star visits your setting. Bear in mind, if they're doing anything other than playing a gig you had better get all kinds of permission before they sue your sorry backside. Or make up a pop star and have all the teens rave about them so the reader gets the picture.

Favourite Quote

FIND A QUOTE, perhaps one of your favourites, and use it as a basis for a short story. You can find quotes online, or I use an app called Quotes.

47

Processing Procession

Walk around the house thinking about your current story. The very fact you are up and moving will allow you to process what you are doing and allow more thoughts to come into your head.

Give Yourself Permission

Give yourself permission to write what you may consider rubbish. Write without thinking about what you are writing, where it is going or fits in. You'll find your brain will have thrown some nuggets of gold in there, nuggets, which are exactly what your story needs. Your brain is a clever organ so give it some free rein and let it strut its stuff.

Sensory Overload

I T ' S time to overload your senses. All of them. At the same time. Burn some citrus incense sticks. Sip from a drink which has a strong taste. Crank up the volume on some music as well as cranking up the lights. Make a conscious effort to feel different textures. Really overload your senses. Once you've done this, turn to writing and see where it takes you once all five senses join in.

IF SENSORY OVERLOAD is difficult for you, please use common sense with this one. I don't want you to be ill.

~

Word Switch

IF YOU HAVE BECOME COMPLETELY STUCK on a specific part of your WIP then rewrite the last three sentences switching new words in for the old ones. This might just be what your brain needs to revitalise it and get it back on track.

~

A Feeling Deep Down

REACH WAY DEEP INSIDE and examine your emotions. How do you feel right now? Why do you feel like that? Is there something bothering you? If not, what is telling you stuck is the place to be at when writing? If you get no answers then fabulous, get writing because you've just proved to your brain that it's fine and dandy and you can write like the bats of hell are coming after you.

Mirror Mirror

LOOK IN THE MIRROR. What do you see? Yourself, Of course that's right but what else do you see? Nothing. I don't believe you. Okay, let me steer you right. You see a writer. A brilliant writer who brings joy to all your readers. You are a truly gifted person and are doing exactly what you should be doing.

Boredom Threshold

HAVE you considered you might be stuck because you are bored with what you are writing? If you are bored, then your reader will be bored too. It's time to go back and read the last three chapters. How can you rewrite them to pick up the pace? The answers as to where you should go next will magically throw themselves at you when you change direction.

48

A Knotty Problem

Teach yourself how to tie a knot. Any type of nautical knot. Whilst you are using the analytical part of your brain the creative part will be churning away in the background, working on the issues in your manuscript.

Art Appreciation

ITEMS NEEDED. Paper. Coloured pens. Adult colouring book.

SPEND the next hour drawing and colouring in. Not only will it help to relax you, you will be stimulating the creative part of your brain, preparing it to develop stories at the right moment.

· · ·

PLUS YOU'LL HAVE a lot of fun in the process.

Let's Start at the Very Beginning – or Not.

IF YOU'RE PARALYSED by first line fear, fear not. There is absolutely no law in the world saying you need to start your novel by writing a killer first line. You obviously want it to have one by the time it's published but that can come later. If you want to start writing the chapter where John and Betty idly chat to the killer whilst doing their weekly shop, then do so. You are in charge. Once you start writing you can worry about a killer first line later.

Make a Difference – Office

FIRSTLY, tidy up your office. If you are anything like me, working in chaos is a creativity killer.

YOU CAN TAKE this one step further by moving your office around if you are able. I can't as my furniture is fixed to the walls, but a different vista can make you think in a different way.

You can also recreate this new vista effect by pinning something different up above your desk.

Plan for a change

PLAN out the next three chapter of your book. Often what paralyses us as writers is the enormity of what we still have to write. If you plan out three chapters at a time this can remove the fear. Planning can also allow you to relax as you now have a structure on which to build your prose.

Hear Here

TIME TO LOOK at words that sound the same but are spelled differently. The nuances of these will be picked up by the brain even if we don't consciously realise it. This can be a good way to engage your readers through slight sleight of hand.

Colour Changing

THIS IS one for a notebook and pen. Actually, a notebook and coloured pens.

WRITE A PARAGRAPH IN ONE COLOUR. Then, write a paragraph in another colour. And another colour. Keep going until you have used all the colours.

LOOK at all those lovely words you've written. I can bet your brain was so busy working out what colour it was going to use next it completely forgot it was stuck.

49

Over to You

Today you are free to choose any activity you want from this book and do it again. Whatever one you felt was the most fun or gave you the greatest boost. Repeat it. Success breeds success.

Writing Prompt

IN THE SPACE below write down the first four words that come into your head. Then use them to form the next part of your storyline, or a short story, poem or flash fiction.

Language Barrier

USE GOOGLE TRANSLATE to translate a couple of paragraphs of

your WIP into another language. Print it out and pin it up above your desk. Imagine what it would be like to have your whole manuscript translated into another language. Hold that thought and use it to motivate you when times are tough. You can't translate a half-finished manuscript as it aint going to sell.

∾

Space Matters

PREVIOUSLY I ENCOURAGED you to move the furniture around in your office. That may be impossible as you are using a small nook. Look at ways you can rearrange your workspace. It may give you an unsettled feel but work with it. The unsettled feeling can be used to good effect by using it to move forward in your project.

∾

Leave Time for Leaves

NOT JUMPING in them this time but spending time looking at the trees and the leaves. I had a forest scene in one of my books. I went to the forest in question and looked at the trees so I could get a more rounded picture of what the scene looked like. I was able to envisage the chase that took place. In another book, I was able to work out exactly where I could bury the body.

NOT THAT I'M encouraging you to kill anyone. This book is not a murderer's training manual.

∾

Perfect Timing

PLAN IN WRITING time for the next week and plan out what you are going to write in each block of time. Having everything scheduled will give your brain time to work out exactly where it is going to go each day.

Coffee Blend

GO OUT TO A NICE CAFÉ, order a cup of coffee and read a good book. It's time for a bit of rest and relaxation.

50

Sensory Overload - Sound Barriers

L isten to as many different sounds as you can on the Internet. Keep going until your brain says no more and then stop. Jot down how you felt listening to each sound. Use some of these in your WIP. For example, bird song, gunshot, tractor, horses, ships horn. This will add realism to any work.

Sniff Sniff

YOU GUESSED IT, we're talking about the sense of smell again today. It's time to overload your sense of smell. Sniff different things in the house and garden. Finish by smelling peppermint, which, I mentioned previously, heightens your creativity. Immediately sit down and start your writing for the day and see how easily and fast those words flow.

Use Your Mince Pies

YES, that's right. The same as the previous two days exercises but overload your eyes with images. You can use books and the Internet for this.

NOW, start writing right now.

Bark is Worse

IF YOU OWN A DOG, take it on a long walk somewhere different. If not, borrow one and take it for a long walk. Notice their actions, the sound of their bark, how they react with people, objects and other animals, the colour of the light on their fur, in fact, everything about them. Jot everything down or dictate it for listening later. Use this to bring sparks of realism into your WIP. The fresh air and exercise will also boost your creativity.

Time for Tea

MAKE your characters sit down and have tea with each other. Write the funniest scene you can possibly imagine.

ONCE YOU HAVE DONE THAT, work out how to make it funnier.

Good for You

Do something today that is good for you either mentally or physically. Take time to look after yourself and your health. If you're run down then you are not going to be functioning well creatively.

Out of Your Comfort Zone - Reading

Go to a bookshop or the library and choose a book that is completely out of your comfort zone reading-wise. Spend an hour reading it and pledge to read it for an hour every day until it is finished. Reading widely makes us much better writers.

51

Country Music

Find some country music on the radio or whatever music player you use. If you are still using CDs then, you guessed it, borrow a country music CD from the library. Spend some time listening to it. You will find the songs are stories in themselves and the beat of the music will boost your creativity.

Pick Up the Pace

SET a timer for thirty minutes and write as fast as you can without stopping. No thinking about it. No editing. Just writing.

YES, I know it seems like a long time but you've been picking up the pace since the beginning of this book, so you're a pro.

Writing Prompt

In her purple dress she...

Rest Up

Have a day off. Rest up. Slob. Watch telly. Do nothing. A little bit of what you fancy does you good.

World Affairs

Read an international newspaper or at least part of one. You can do this online. It is good to look at news from a different perspective. It is human nature to view things through our own lenses, so borrowing someone else's can give you a broader picture. Also, you might find a line or a couple of sentences give you and idea of where to go next in your WIP.

I Bet you Can

I bet you can write one sentence.

I bet you can write one paragraph.

. . .

I BET you can write one chapter.

I KNOW you can write this book.

How Tall

NO GOING out and climbing buildings or hills this time. Do some research on the tallest things in your area. The tallest building. The tallest person in your city. The tallest monument. The tallest hill. At the end of it, you'll know more than you did to start with and you can now use one of them to move your WIP forward. There has to be some sort of know it all in your book who would drop this sort of titbit in at the most inopportune moment.

52

Movie Madness

Watch a movie in the same genre that you are writing. Analyse it for the way in which they have your emotions rising and falling. Analyse the parts where they have you on the edge of the seat and wondering what comes next. Use these techniques to help you develop your novel and lift up that infernal saggy middle.

Eleven Fingers

GIVE one of your characters an unusual physical trait. Much better than my eleven fingers of the title. Think of ways in which you can use this as a plot twist. I can tell you I've a cracker in mind at the moment.

Head Space

JUST AS YOU needhead space to clear your head and recharge, so do your characters. You may be stuck because the poor souls are exhausted and refusing to play ball. Do something fun with them, even in the midst of a tense situation. At least give the poor soul time to drink a beer or eat a burger.

Touchy Feely

No, no, no. Not that way. You'll get arrested. Make a concerted effort to use your sense of touch today. I know you've done this previously but heightening all your senses can make you much more aware of your surroundings and make you a better writer.

Pristine White

TAKE a nice white sheet of paper and draw a doodle at the top of it. Now it's not a blank piece of paper any more, write something about the doodle. Staring at a blank sheet is never a good idea, so do anything to make sure it's not blank anymore. Your brain can sigh and relax.

There's Nothing New

AS THE SAYING GOES, there is nothing new. Many writers get hung up in the middle of their book as they feel it's all been done before. You're right, it has been done before. But not the way you are doing it. Every writer puts his or her own unique spin on a story and you are no different. In fact, you are uniquely you and that is what makes this book so brilliant.

Take My Hand

IN A METAPHORICAL SENSE OF COURSE. I am right there beside you cheering you on. Who else has their own personal cheerleader on the sidelines urging them to take one more step? You have almost completed 366 exercises, which has helped you to develop as a writer and develop your creativity. You are a truly great writer and I believe in you.

53

Live From

Anywhere you want. Think of the place you would really like to write today and go there. Within reason of course. I would rather like to write at the top of the Statue of Liberty today but as I live in Scotland it might be a tad difficult. The world is your oyster so go wherever you want to go.

~

Shut Down

SHUT down the computer and take a day off. That's it. No suggestions or ideas, just a day off. You know just the right thing to do to get those creative juices flowing and your heart rate jumping.

~

Sunshine

Go out into the sunshine and write. Given the terrible ability of computer screens to be unreadable in bright light this will involve taking a paper and pen. Sunshine always makes one feel much better and think of all that lovely Vitamin D. Do wear sunscreen though as sunburn really saps your creativity.

Windblown

More of the elements. Go for a long walk in the wind. Yes, this is a repeat but it bears repeating as it really does blow the cobwebs away. If it's the calmest day of the year for you and there's not a breath of wind, stand in front of a fan going at full blast and use that brilliant imagination of yours to picture a howling gale. Now, take your characters into a similar weather pattern.

Late Night

Many people write first thing in the morning, as they are less tired and feel they are more creative. Have you tried working late at night? You may be surprised at how much you actually get done. You will find your brain has been percolating ideas all day and they are ripe for the pouring.

So, off you go and pour - all those bright, shiny excitable words on to the page. You're a true pro at this now and will write more than your wild dreams could conjure up.

Spare Change

GATHER TOGETHER every piece of spare change you have in the house. Take it along to a local charity and give it to them. What has this got to do with creativity? Not much, as it happens, but you will feel good about it and that is always a good thing. You will also have helped someone much less fortunate than you.

Favourite Things

THINK of all your favourite things. Choose three of them and promise you can have them when you've written ten chapters. Don't cheat and do reward yourself. If one of them happens to be an around the world trip, don't forget your laptop.

It's a Wrap

CONGRATULATIONS YOU'VE REACHED day 366. Give yourself a pat on the back and a loud cheer. You are a winner and you can win at writing too.

54

CONCLUSION

I started this book saying this was the beginning of a new adventure to a place where your writing mojo would come winging its way back. *You* started this book a year ago, full of hope and excitement, knowing your journey would be revolutionised one creative step at a time. Look back over the past year and take stock of how much you've achieved. Please note, I am not saying you are at the end of the journey because you are not. This is only the beginning. A glorious future beckons. One where writing is a joy, rather than a challenge. Where you rush towards creating, rather than viewing it as a chore.

NOW YOU ARE GLORIOUSLY unstuck you know what you should do to move it forward if you ever find yourself slipping again. Also, dipping in and out of the challenges and doing them again, will give you fresh insight every single time.

· · ·

I WILL FINISH by saying all the very best with your writing. I can't wait to read your books.

ABOUT THE AUTHOR

Wendy H. Jones is a writer of adult crime, cozy mysteries, young adult mysteries and children's picture books. She is an international public speaker and runs motivational, marketing and writing workshops. She uses her NLP training to help authors develop marketing techniques and revolutionise the way in which they approach writing. She combines this with her love of travel and meeting new people.

ALSO BY WENDY H. JONES

Non-Fiction

Power Packed Book Marketing

DI Shona McKenzie Mysteries

Killer's Countdown

Killer's Craft

· Killer's Cross

Killer's Cut

Killer's Crew

Killer's Crypt

Cass Claymore Investigates

Antiques and Alibis

The Fergus and Flora Mysteries

The Dagger's Curse

The Haunted Broch

Children's Picture Books

Bertie the Buffalo

Lightning Source UK Ltd.
Milton Keynes UK
UKHW021106101219
355113UK00009B/303/P